Quiz 2000
No. 1

Roy Ward Dickson

D1078798

Wolfe

First published 1975 by Wolfe Publishing Limited
10 Earlham Street, London WC2H 9BR

Titles in this Series:

QUIZ 2000 *1*   SBN 7234 0578 6
QUIZ 2000 *2*   SBN 7234 0579 4
QUIZ 2000 *3*   SBN 7234 0580 8
QUIZ 2000 *4*   SBN 7234 0581 6

Made and printed in Great Britain by
C. Nicholls & Company Ltd.

INTRODUCTION

Following the huge success of 'The Greatest Quiz Book Ever'*, with its challenging quizzes on dozens of *individual* subjects, I was asked to put together a whole series of slightly simpler *general knowledge* quiz books, to be published in handy 'pocket' size.

This is one of them, and I'm confident that you'll enjoy it, and the others in the series.

Scores of over 30 (per 50-question quiz) are good. Over 40, excellent. Over 45, outstanding.

The answers are given, in sequence, from page 75.

Have fun — and, when you're through with it, why not pass the book along to a 'shut-in', or someone in hospital?

*Wolfe Publishing £2.50   Roy Ward Dickson

QUIZ 1

1. Of what article of apparel did Sir Winston Churchill amass a considerable collection?
2. Of what type of metal are most church-bells fabricated?
3. Another name for lockjaw?
4. Who, and in what country, were killed in large numbers on St Bartholomew's Day?
5. Which is not part of one's body — radius, scapula, sphincter, spatula, ventricle?
6. Name the 'Benelux' countries.
7. What is spermaceti?
8. What is most likely the oldest sport?
9. Who, for many years, was the communist leader of North Vietnam?
10. What is Jutland?
11. 'Admissible' or 'admissable'?
12. People of — where? — refer to their area as 'Bayern'.
13. 'One, two, three, kick.' What dance does that suggest?
14. What's a katydid?
15. Which is the land of the Khmer people?
16. Are all sharks dangerous to Man?
17. If Britain's next female sovereign chose the name Mary, what, numerically speaking, would she be called?
18. What is leprosy now called?
19. Belleek. A type of carpet, lace, or china?
20. Rearrange the name of a famous English poet into the name of an English composer.
21. Officially, who was it who was called 'Rufus'?
22. What's another name for ascorbic acid?
23. Are oysters the only creatures that form pearls?
24. What is nacre?
25. What, specifically, are sinuses?
26. Which country has, by far, the greatest number of lakes?
27. The word for a vertical window projecting from a sloping roof?
28. Is Ajaccio in France, Italy, or Spain?
29. Does 'pugilist' come from a word meaning fist, fight, or wager?
30. What is grosgrain?
31. What's unusual about the word 'cleave'?
32. The word for a poem narrating heroic achievements or historic events?
33. Which eggs are, normally, largest — hens', ducks', or those of geese?

4

34. Has Holland any mountains at all?

35. What, notably, is Dunnet Head?

36. Who was Prospero's 'savage and deformed slave'?

37. Give two meanings of the word 'moccasin'.

38. Who was Lev Bronstein?

39. Which is the largest animal of the deer family?

40. What do most of us eat that has already been eaten once?

41. Is stramonium a plant used in medicine, a rare metal, or an old-fashioned musical instrument?

42. A healthy man of thirty marries a healthy woman of forty. Which can, actuarily, expect to outlive the other?

43. Which has a movable crest of feathers — the cockatoo, the macaw, the parrot, the love-bird, or the budgerigar?

44. What would one plant in a trundle-bed?

45. Rome has always been the home of whom?

46. Give at least three different exceptions to the 'i' before 'e' except after 'c' spelling rule.

47. You could be forgiven for thinking a gavial was a — what?

48. For what country did the British North America Act serve as a 'constitution'?

49. How many plays are wholly or collaboratively credited to William Shakespeare? 23 — 38 — or 47?

50. What famous artists's surname was Buonarroti?

QUIZ 2

1. What's the difference between the ways that recumbent horses and cows get up?

2. What does the first 'S' in USSR stand for?

3. Who was called 'The Great Commoner' — William Pitt the Elder, William Pitt the younger, or Oliver Cromwell?

4. Is a Madeira cake plain, fruity, or soaked in wine?

5. In what country did skiing first become a sport?

6. Do any 'jellyfish' grow to more than 20 feet in length?

7. What famous airship was named after an elderly field-marshal?

8. Who organised a famous rebellion of gladiators and slaves against Rome in 73 BC?

9. What does the phrase 'ad hoc' mean?

10. Where was the body of Henry Hudson, the explorer, found?

11. When two circles, on the same plane, intersect, must they invariably do so in just two places?

12. To whom do we owe 'The Moon and Sixpence'?

13. Why, in North America, is a quarter-dollar coin familiarly known as 'two bits'?
14. If Simple Simon didn't steal the pig, who did?
15. What does a Protestant arrow-maker have in common with the leader of the Bounty mutineers?
16. To whom, as a church, was Westminster Abbey dedicated?
17. Did William Shakespeare actually attend a school?
18. What are the two elements of which ammonia (not in solution) is composed?
19. It's a common belief that the ratio of male babies born in belligerent countries, during a war, increases. True?
20. Another name for a stomach ulcer?
21. Do any fish bear live young?
22. What's the word for a prong of a fork? And the word for a prong of a deer's antler?
23. What part of the plant is the clove we use as a spice?
24. Bombay was part of the dowry of the queen of what British ruler?
25. Is there actually a 'castle' or palace at 'Elsinore' (Haelsingor)?
26. Who wrote 'King Solomon's Mines'?
27. The word for delicate, lace-like, ornamental work done with fine gold or silver wire?
28. In Spain, notably, the older lady who acts as a chaperon is called a — what?
29. What does a 'ghost-writer' do?
30. What does 'auto-' at the beginning of a word mean?
31. With what bird is the halcyon usually identified?
32. What's Africa's highest peak?
33. By what name is the great Venetian painter, T. Vecellio, better known?
34. What are anadromous fish?
35. Of what was Somnus the god?
36. What animal has the most affirmative-sounding name?
37. What extension, to one side, do many native canoes in the South Pacific have?
38. Distinguish between 'fluid' and 'liquid'.
39. Name Sindbad the Sailor's enormous bird.
40. What's a peavey used for?
41. How many men have been known to run (for a short distance) at 30 mph or better?
42. If you found a few pignolias in your pocket, what might you be excused for exclaiming?
43. What's Mariolatry?

44. Where should guppies be kept?
45. From what generic group of fruits are the majority of marmalades made?
46. What famous artist's alliterative first names were those of two of the bible's saints?
47. Was Sir Winston Churchill ever awarded a Nobel Prize, and, if so, for — what?
48. Where is Rotorua, and what makes it famous? (Full answer.)
49. What country's flag is a yellow off-centre cross with a blue 'background'?
50. These splendid sights are all in which of the United States? The Grand Canyon, the Petrified Forest, The Painted Desert, and Meteor Crater.

QUIZ 3

1. Does the Equator run through Kenya?
2. What is husbandry?
3. How high was the famous Colossus of Rhodes — about 105 feet, 205, or 305?
4. Which is the further south — Rangoon or Mandalay?
5. What was the ancient belief involving salamanders and fire?
6. Which of the gospels do we owe to John the Baptist?
7. What long narrow archipelago extends westward from Alaska?
8. 'There's a divinity that shapes our — what?' A line from what play? (Full answer.)
9. Valentina Tereshkova married Andreyan Nikolayev. Both were noted as — what?
10. Minorca is part of what island group?
11. How many times was Abraham Lincoln elected president of his country?
12. What was Rembrandt's first name?
13. What's the world's SECOND highest mountain (from sea level)?
14. Is 'apothecary' an old name for a lawyer?
15. Did Sir Humphry Davy perform experiments in connection with photography?
16. All of us in broadcasting love to have fans. Where did that word 'fan' come from?
17. There's a long-snouted, long-tailed, raccoon-like creature called a coati. Its full name?

18. With what activity do we associate the name of Hippocrates?
19. What artist is credited with inventing the wheelbarrow?
20. What common vegetable gets its name from a word meaning 'big head'?
21. What's baccarat?
22. 'Ye olde Coffee Shoppe'. How, correctly, was the 'ye' pronounced?
23. Johann Sebastian Bach's son Johann was also an organist and composer, and lived for a while in England. What was his middle name?
24. Whose brother was Aaron?
25. What famous statesman is buried at Hyde Park, New York (State)?
26. What was once treated with chaulmoogra oil?
27. Who succeeded William and Mary as sovereign?
28. What's the all-inclusive term for what's placed under (say) a bar in order to use it as a lever?
29. During which war did Florence Nightingale gain fame?
30. Which side of the brain controls functions of the left side of the body?
31. How did Rasputin, the Mad Monk of Russia, die?
32. What substance is used to 'make visible' the lines of force of a magnet?
33. Is chickenpox spread by chickens?
34. The Pied Piper of ——?
35. What instrument measures wind velocity?
36. What's baksheesh?
37. Reverse a word meaning 'certain skin growths', into one meaning 'dry cereal stalks'.
38. For what Latin phrase is NB ('note well') an abbreviation?
39. In what mountains is the famous Kicking Horse Pass?
40. What's meant by dying intestate?
41. Which of her relatives did Cleopatra marry?
42. A fancier word for homesickness?
43. The name Jean Henri Fabre is particularly associated with the study of what creatures?
44. What late film star is best remembered for his portrayals of Sherlock Holmes?
45. (3 seconds.) Which letter of the alphabet takes longest to say?
46. Hats predominantly made in one country are named for what country further north?

47. Iron pyrites has misled many people. Hence, what popular name for it?

48. What large black birds are associated with the Tower of London?

49. What country was first mistakenly named by the Portuguese, 'island of the True Cross'?

50. 'Divers', of course, dive. What else does the word mean?

QUIZ 4

1. What, if anything, do penguins use their wings for?

2. Name the great peasant soup of Italy.

3. What percentage of divorced persons re-marry within five years — 19, 37, 73?

4. What was the first missile to be fired by means of gunpowder (at least in Europe)?

5. What are 'tangerine oranges' from the Orient usually called?

6. Name the nearest star.

7. What would happen if a venomous snake actually bit a mongoose?

8. What kind of material is made from the skin of ostriches?

9. If currants were named for Corinth, how did raisins get their name?

10. Do all living plants contain chlorophyll?

11. Biblically, who was the first person to see a rainbow?

12. Who or what is Anisette?

13. What was the work engaged in by St Matthew (Levi) prior to his becoming an apostle?

14. If the St Lawrence isn't Canada's longest river, what is?

15. Wales was Cambria. What was Portugal?

16. Who are advised to study the ways of an ant?

17. What law prevented France's ever being ruled by a queen?

18. What's the meaning of the doggy name 'Fido'?

19. Who seek Nirvana?

20. 'Acid' is sour. What's 'acrid'?

21. In what year did the Bolshevik revolution take place?

22. What was the former name of Botswana?

23. What famous thoroughfare extended from Lashio to Kunming?

24. Did Canute ever rule over England and Denmark simultaneously?

25. Where is Tananarive?

26. Which came first — the reputed days of King Arthur or the erecting of Stonehenge?

27. The so-called 'grass skirts' worn by Pacific islanders are usually made of leaf-strips from what tree?
28. Do turtles lay their eggs ashore, or on the sea-bottom — and do they 'sit' on them? (Full answer.)
29. What gives red grape wines their colour?
30. Apart from Victoria, who reigned in Britain the longest?
31. What normally solid element appears to be absolutely essential to all plant and animal tissues?
32. Of what is 1.723 (approximately) the square root?
33. In humans which is usually finer, blond hair or dark?
34. What word is applied, collectively, to the internal-secreting glands (e.g. thyroid, pineal, pituitary)?
35. Does the entire 180th meridian serve as the International Date Line?
36. Who became first Earl of Beaconsfield?
37. Describe (a) the colour, (b) the odour, of pure oxygen.
38. Two poker players hold and show royal flushes, one in hearts, one in spades. Which one wins?
39. Which sex, among birds, is predominantly the more brightly-coloured?
40. What creatures belong to the ophidian sub-order of reptiles?
41. What does one 'plant', to grow mushrooms?
42. A good four-man team of Australian sheep-shearers can shear how many sheep in a normal day's work — about 80, 160, or over 500?
43. A dory could be either of what two things associated with water? (Full answer.)
44. Correctly pronounce 'victuals'.
45. What's the predominant religion of Pakistan?
46. What did alienists specialise in?
47. Geographically, what's an enclave?
48. In what river is the large island called Anticosti?
49. A diamond weighs 1.34 carats. 34 what?
50. Which late great star gave a magnificent film portrayal of Benjamin Disraeli?

QUIZ 5
1. In what well-known building was Sir Winston Churchill born?
2. 'Poly' means 'many'. What's polydactyly?
3. What substance is not solid at absolute zero?
4. Within two, about how many inches of snow make one inch of water?

5. What combination of three colours is commonest among national flags?
6. Are translucent substances transparent or opaque?
7. To the reign of which king, particularly, does 'Jacobean' refer?
8. How was the original 'Peeping Tom' punished?
9. Name the two American coastal states that each consist mainly of an enormous peninsula.
10. Goldfish are actually a variety of what fish?
11. Did Britain ever have a Prime Minister named Robert Eden?
12. Baby seals are called — what?
13. What name is commonly given to infectious parotitis?
14. What non-military organisation bases its motto on preparedness?
15. The New Hebrides were given joint administration by France and Britain. What's this sort of arrangement called?
16. Does it take more or less heat to boil water at the bottom of a deep mine-shaft?
17. Do weeping willows prefer wet or dry growing conditions?
18. Of what is this sentence an example: 'Fifty Frenchmen found Fred's fat frogs fine food?'
19. What is the world's tallest mountain 'peak', measured from its submarine base?
20. What reptilian lachrymatory manifestation signifies insincerity in the expression of grief?
21. Which is the heavier, helium or hydrogen?
22. What, originally, was a pastor?
23. Name at least five of the six fields in which Nobel prizes are awarded.
24. In three seconds: how many months have a 'g' in their name?
25. (10 secs.) Ignoring names, what two consecutively-sounded letters of the alphabet, form an English word?
26. The Friendly Islands are probably now better known as— what?
27. What would a person do, if anything, with a burnoose?
28. Wolfram is a rarely-used name for what important metal?
29. Film-world question. A.K. wed M.O. Who were they?
30. Who commanded the Grand Fleet at the battle of Jutland?
31. Substitution of a related word, as in 'the turf' for horse-racing, is called simile, metaphor, or metonymy. Which?
32. Who was Walter Tell?
33. To what country do the Faröe Islands belong?

11

34. Who was the last King of Egypt?
35. In what position do horses usually sleep?
36. Reseda is grown more for its fragrance than its looks. Better known name for it?
37. What tiny country, rarely in the news, is tucked between Switzerland and Austria?
38. We eat the root of Zinziber officinale. What is it?
39. Assuming cloudless weather — when can one see furthest— 11 am, 5 pm, or 3 am?
40. What buildings are most likely to have minarets?
41. Does the USA share any part of the St Lawrence River with Canada?
42. What valuable animals breed in the Pribilov Islands (North Pacific)? Why valuable? (Full answer.)
43. What was the most notable thing about the manner of Uriah Heep?
44. What and where are these: Dniepr, Dniestr?
45. Does wood have to be specially treated to become teak?
46. What fruit is most closely related to almonds?
47. 'The House of — how many — Gables?'
48. Who was Sherlock Holmes' constantly astonished friend?
49. What famous ursine creatures discovered an intruder of a different species?
50. Reverse a word meaning 'a tiny insect', into one meaning 'pleasantly penetrating flavour'.

QUIZ 6
1. What calendar month, more often than not, approximately matches a lunar month in duration?
2. Who painted 'The Age of Innocence'?
3. What are the Dodecanese?
4. How many major *classes* of vertebrates (e.g. mammals) are there?
5. Assuming both were record-holders, who could expect to win a 200 metre race between a sprinter and a skater?
6. At what age, in months, do human molar teeth normally start to appear — 15, 30, or 60?
7. The first land sighted by Columbus was an island in the Bahamas (Watling Island.) What did he call it?
8. Who wrote 'Westward Ho!'?
9. Where did dead Viking heroes go, to feast with Odin?
10. Where is a prophet said to be without honour?
11. To whom do we owe the famous 'Merry Widow' waltz?
12. What are ratlines?

13. Who was Virgil Grissom?
14. When is tea served in a demi-tasse?
15. Name a well-known and handsome, flowering plant, ending with '—yllis'.
16. If you're like most of us, where do you keep your patellae?
17. What Egyptian city was founded by and named after a Macedonian conqueror?
18. Do birds and fishes have nostrils?
19. What do people mean by the initials 'D.g.'?
20. Which has been the more revered — the ibex or the ibis?
21. What's oakum?
22. In what city was John Cabot born?
23. How many black keys in a standard piano keyboard?
24. Who was the first English king to be addressed as 'Your Majesty?'
25. What does he steal 'who steals my purse'?
26. Does Australia proper have any mountains over 7500 feet high?
27. What's unusual about the heads of female reindeer?
28. In what country is the source of Russia's Volga River?
29. What's the all-too-common error in the pronunciation of 'government'?
30. Apart from the nine planets, their moons, Saturn's ring, and comets, what else is orbiting about the Sun?
31. On what part of their anatomy did women wear bustles?
32. Who was America's best-known Mamie?
33. Which month was named for the Roman god of war?
34. Can hens lay shell-less eggs?
35. Where would you find an ulna?
36. What hibernating rodent, not unfamiliar to Britons, could be called 'halfway between a mouse and a squirrel'?
37. On the border between Peru and Bolivia is the world's highest steam-navigated lake. Name it.
38. Which is the largest species of ape?
39. Where is Malaga, famous for its grapes and wine?
40. What's danced to 'three-quarter' time?
41. How much gold is now produced in the non-communist world annually — about 200 tons, 1,500 tons, or 30,000 tons?
42. Who was Rudolph Valentino, and what was his national origin? (Full answer).
43. Where is Darwin (place, not person)?
44. What, in everyday English, do we call the Palaeolithic Age?
45. What was Einstein's first name?

46. Sneeze the name of a nut.

47. A Frenchman reciting the alphabet would call which letter 'Eegreck'?

48. What strait separates Siberia from Alaska?

49. In what year was John F. Kennedy assassinated?

50. Correctly pronounce 'ribald'.

QUIZ 7

1. California has a magnificent national park named — what? — for the fantastic giant redwood trees there.

2. Has there ever been a dead heat in the Oxford-Cambridge Boat Race?

3. Birds have nictitating membranes, each serving as a third — what?

4. Removing the water content from a substance is called — what? ('Drying' won't do.)

5. Before the discovery of petroleum, what kind of oil was most commonly burned in lampoons?

6. What does a carilloneur do?

7. A thickened soup, made with puréed tomato and, say, crab, shrimp or lobster, is called a — what?

8. What was the surname of the father and son who both served as presidents of the US?

9. What event in 1605 is best remembered by British schoolboys?

10. With what did the name Baedeker become associated?

11. Which country gave its name to a bird that's actually native to a faraway continent?

12. Which means 'every two years' — biennial, or biannual?

13. Noyau is a liqueur. Flavoured with what?

14. Is nutmeg obtained from a vine, a tree, or a shrub?

15. Did the French admiral Darlan die from old age, in battle, or by assassination?

16. Who was the best-known person to bear the surname Alighieri?

17. Which state of the USA has at least 56 mountain peaks 14,000 or more feet high?

18. What, to a horse, is a calk?

19. Has there ever been a genuine case of somnambulism?

20. Who's the best-known Briton to have borne the first names 'Herbert Henry'?

21. What are astute people?

22. If a newt loses a leg, can it grow a new one?

23. Who was called the 'Tiger of France'?

24. Which way do convex lenses bulge, inward or outward?
25. Amber is fossilised — what?
26. What colour of light is used to indicate the starboard side?
27. Do orthodox Jews count the years from the birth of Moses, the death of Abraham, or the 'creation of the world'?
28. Handel's name was originally Haendel. What was his full name?
29. An ichneumon fly is an insect related to the wasp — but what's an ichneumon?
30. What's the term for that branch of chemistry concerned with compounds of carbon?
31. Do reindeer shed their antlers?
32. Evaporation from what helps dogs to cool off?
33. What's the word for the tree-sap from which rubber is made?
34. Is there any chlorine in chloroform?
35. Which two of Canada's 10 provinces are widely known by their initials. (Full answer.)
36. In what famous novel was there a character named Steerforth?
37. What distinguishes a rebus from a conundrum?
38. What holiday always falls on a Friday?
39. Who was the first man on the Moon?
40. Is the Danube actually blue?
41. In what country is the famous Aletsch Glacier?
42. Did people wear, spend, or recite doubloons?
43. In Marseilles, especially, you are likely to be served a stew-like soup, full of fish and shellfish, called — what?
44. What was buna-S?
45. What's a shad?
46. What's gouache?
47. What's the word for the French-speaking segment of Belgium's population?
48. Which tree's name sounds like a machine used by farmers?
49. What that you could hold in your hand, besides insects, are called locusts?
50. A familiar first name for a girl, ending in 'cent'?

QUIZ 8
1. What is supposed to have been used by Cleopatra to commit suicide?
2. The main vein of precious metal being mined in a given area is referred to as — what?
3. If a bambino isn't a short bamboo pole, what is it?

4. How often, in an average century, can Easter Sunday fall on 26 April?
5. What's an amnesty?
6. What was the name of the winged horse of mythology?
7. What's the word for a planned (or recorded) route of travel?
8. Strictly speaking, what's the difference in origin between vellum and parchment?
9. Name any two consecutive months with 31 days in them.
10. Princess Sophia of Anhalt-Zerbst is better remembered as whom?
11. Name the silkworm's favourite food.
12. If Lake Superior is not the world's deepest lake, what is?
13. Is a porbeagle a shark, a dog, or a trap for eagles?
14. D.P. are the initials for what fierce breed of dog?
15. Who was William the Conqueror's mother?
16. What surname was shared by the brothers Dante Gabriel— and William Michael —?
17. What shape is an acre?
18. What did Richard II have in common with Edward VIII?
19. Strictly speaking, is jaundice a disease or a symptom?
20. Were all Archbishops of Canterbury, since the Norman Conquest, born in Britain?
21. Aristotle is said firmly to have believed that what could be spontaneously generated in the carcass of an ox?
22. At what speed, approximately, did the Wright Brothers' first aeroplane fly — 10, 30, or 62 miles per hour?
23. What country, for a while, had a 'parliament' called the Duma?
24. Which is or are caused by a virus — measles, mumps, 'scarlet fever', whooping-cough?
25. Was the Armada defeated in 1555, 1558, or 1588?
26. Did Prince Charles receive part of his formal schooling in Australia?
27. Who were called black friars?
28. What do plagiarists do?
29. Of what was Pluto the god?
30. Muscat and — what?
31. Who led Alice into Wonderland?
32. What's the name (now) of the famous, huge, deep blue diamond long believed to have brought ill fortune to its owner?
33. What are pyrotechnics?

34. Whose inheritance cannot be superseded by the birth of another — an heir apparent or presumptive?
35. Of whom or what is 'Domine Dirige Nos' the motto?
36. What military unit does a colonel normally command?
37. Distinguish between 'bort' and 'borscht'. (Full answer.)
38. The capital of what country is nearest Latitude zero, Longitude zero?
39. What connection is there between eggs and tennis?
40. Which may weigh more, a featherweight, or a flyweight, boxer?
41. Another name for hoarfrost?
42. What sport, popular among western Americans, is sometimes called 'barnyard golf'?
43. Where's Gander?
44. Spell the name of the best-known extinct flying reptile.
45. A jalousie is a kind of — what?
46. Deliberate inoculation with what mild disease generates immunity to smallpox?
47. Of what are 'neurons' the basic structural unit?
48. What is food served 'en coquille'?
49. The names of three of the best-known ranges of hills in England have what in common?
50. Name a disease, ending in 'x', that can be passed on to Man by animal-bristles or wool.

QUIZ 9

1. To a hungry Italian, what is 'pizzicato'?
2. Which planet has a moon called Hades?
3. How many hams would fourteen pigs provide?
4. The origin of 'Anzac', please.
5. Venice had its Doge. What did Genoa have?
6. What is it that these cities have in common — or, rather, don't have — Hull, Plymouth, Cambridge?
7. An American tells a Cockney to 'pipe down', and is in turn advised to 'belt up'! Are their suggestions identical?
8. From what language do we get the word 'pyjamas'?
9. What word is applied to deliberately formed, complicated, chemically joined, 'chains' of molecules of a simpler substance?
10. When sailors 'splice the mainbrace', what are they doing?
11. What are hares called in North America?
12. What one country occupies about 90 per cent of the Arabian Peninsula?

13. How many earthquakes (or tremors) has Britain experienced during the past 1000 years? (Within 50 per cent.)

14. What modern English word (apart from I) can be spelled out as a correct arrangement of Roman numerals?

15. What was the Holy Grail, supposedly sought by Arthur's knights?

16. Albrecht Dürer is famous for — what?

17. Another name for rabies?

18. Name a sin that's not a crime.

19. Was the word 'Cellophane' trade-marked?

20. What is La Manche?

21. Of what was Bacchus the god?

22. Precious stones are sometimes formed and polished into a smooth rounded rather than a faceted shape. What is such a stone called?

23. What four-legged creatures are most frequently associated with the Galapagos Islands?

24. Locate the famous 'Sugar Loaf' Mountain.

25. If pumice is porous volcanic stone, what's pomace?

26. What, involving time, caused riots in 1752?

27. What poem did Coleridge say came to him in a dream? Hint: K.

28. Is a fugue a wine-vat, a bad smell, or a type of musical composition?

29. Did anyone before Charles Darwin suggest that modern life-forms evolved from earlier ones?

30. What's unusual, but not unique, about the cities of Minneapolis and St Paul, in Minnesota, USA?

31. What name was given the year between 1 BC and 1 AD?

32. Do peanut plants blossom above or below ground?

33. On which side did Holland take part during World War I?

34. Name a South American country that has no coastline.

35. What's the main ingredient of snuff?

36. What were destroyers originally built to attack?

37. Of what was 'Mrs.' originally an abbreviation?

38. Was St Crispin the patron saint of wine-makers, tax-collectors, or shoe-makers?

39. The umbrella's name suggests protection from — what?

40. Would one drink hyson, chase it, or report it to one's doctor?

41. What do fish keep in their bladders?

42. Is belladonna a drug, a singer, a dancer, or a Spanish beauty?

43. Another word for a 'maze'?

44. After Queen Liliuokalani, the last ruler of Hawaii, was deposed, what — notably — did she write?
45. In participating in what sport did 'Babe' Ruth become an American folk hero?
46. With what do many bears satisfy their 'sweet tooth'?
47. What is the attitude of devout Mohammedans towards Abraham?
48. Which is the land of the black swan?
49. What's holystone used for?
50. You find yourself faced with a timbale. What to do?

QUIZ 10

1. How many vessels constituted the Armada — 87, 130, 230, or over 400?
2. 'Blest be the man that spares these stones, and curst be he that moves my bones.' Whose bones?
3. How did our 'question mark' originate?
4. 'But we hae meat, an' we can eat, and sae — — — —'?
5. What's a plebiscite?
6. After whom was the capital city of Saskatchewan named?
7. The dung-beetle was revered in Egypt as a symbol of resurrection. It's better known as what?
8. By what name is the dangerous Ursus horribilis better known?
9. Does Ireland's River Shannon have more or less than 40 tributaries?
10. Which is the windward — the direction in which, or from which, the wind is blowing?
11. What's an abattoir?
12. Should an aquarium be kept in sunlight or in the shade?
13. Did the 'Holy Roman Empire' ever reach the shore of the Baltic?
14. We all know what a peninsula is, but what does the word literally imply?
15. What destroyed Pompeii?
16. What now well-known heavenly body was discovered in 1930 at Flagstaff Observatory, Arizona?
17. Great excitement occurred when a live coelacanth was found. Why?
18. What adjective could be appropriately applied to a written or spoken cliché?
19. Locate the country where the Boxer Rebellion occurred.
20. What's the word for 'stopping up' the seams of a ship?
21. What produces shellac?

22. Which kind of frog nurses its young?
23. Elaborate and brilliant hand decoration of a manuscript (as frequently seen on mediaeval documents) is called what?
24. What was the name of the explorer who first set sail for the west from Bristol, in a ship called the 'Mathew'?
25. Who was Caedmon?
26. In which London park is there a famous statue of one of Sir James M. Barrie's characters?
27. What's a pipkin?
28. From what did John Steinbeck get his book title 'Of Mice and Men'?
29. Which are smallest — chaffinches, wrens, or hummingbirds?
30. What's wrong with mendacious people?
31. When are Hawaiians' floral neck-garlands called 'poi'?
32. In a non-leapyear, which months are more than three days longer than the shortest one?
33. In two or three words, how did 'Lawrence of Arabia' die?
34. Is Brie a famous type of lace, cheese, wine, or pottery?
35. Who was Mickey Mouse's girl friend?
36. 'Bible', literally, means — what?
37. Who is reputed to have been the first queen in the British Isles to wear silk stockings?
38. What common plant got its name from a carnivore's dental equipment?
39. How many ships, as a rule, constituted an argosy?
40. If the lead in a lead pencil isn't lead, as some would lead us to believe, what is it?
41. How many legs can a pair of normal flies honestly claim to possess, between them?
42. What's the difference between a tiller and a rudder?
43. Of what kind of tissue does one's heart predominantly consist?
44. Hera was a sister and wife of Zeus. Who was her Roman counterpart?
45. Where was the Bedlington terrier developed?
47. Water from the mighty Colorado River flows into what ocean?
47. Who, or what, was 'the Brown Bomber'?
48. The sites of the famous Phoenician ports are now within what country?
49. What is the useful gelatinous substance, agar-agar, obtained from?

50. What's wrong, astronomically, with the depiction on a flag of a star within the curve of a crescent moon?

QUIZ 11

1. The famous Egyptian Sphinx has the head of what kind of creature?
2. What's a herbicide?
3. The author, please, of 'Rupert of Hentzau'?
4. Ceres is usually depicted holding a — what?
5. What's Surtsey?
6. What are cabobs?
7. Where are Brunei and Sarawak?
8. How do reptiles differ from us with regard to body temperature?
9. Which is the tropic in the Southern Hemisphere?
10. Distinguish between the studies respectively called anatomy and physiology.
11. What sovereign in this century threatened to create enough extra peers to ensure passage of a liberal piece of legislation?
12. How did all those soluble minerals get into sea water?
13. What, mainly, gives blood its distinctive colour?
14. Does the Sun ever shine on the South Pole?
15. What fraction of a nautical mile is a 'cable'?
16. Are there any volcanoes in North America?
17. What do quinine, cork, and cinnamon have in common?
18. Catherine wheels are fireworks, but, originally, were — what?
19. Who was Britain's first Labour Prime Minister?
20. What did the Luddites smash, and why?
21. From what article do we get the word 'oval'?
22. What is meant by 'Sheffield plate'?
23. Which famous poet was the son of an MP for Shoreham?
24. Why are plants and animals scientifically named in Latin?
25. What's inflamed when one has nephritis?
26. 'Running amok (amuck)'. Is 'amok' a Malay word, German, or Anglo-Saxon?
27. 'The evil that men do oft lives after them'. Which Shakespearian character said it?
28. Add an 'l' to the word for a boat, and get a peak.
29. His name suggests flight, and that's what he did over both Poles. Who?
30. What are Mendelian laws concerned with?

31. What birds commonly 'feed' (partly) on the nectar of certain types of blossoms?
32. When at home, in what country do most Andalusians live?
33. What's a teamed pair of oxen usually called?
34. What's the word usually applied to ridges of rocks and gravel accumulated and deposited by glaciers?
35. What's 'worth two in the bush'?
36. Could a normal healthy man's shinbone support a ton of weight?
37. Where is the poet Dante buried — Ravenna, Pisa, or Florence?
38. What fate once befell both Britain and Sicily?
39. Rhizome, bulb, tuber, corm. Apply those words correctly to these four — iris, jonquil, dahlia, gladiolus.
40. Where are beavers marsupials?
41. Which is the particularly vain one — an egoist or an egotist?
42. Do more, or less, than ten unrelated English words commence with a silent 'k'?
43. In whose reign did the Maundy Money custom commence?
44. Generally, which eagles fly off seeking food for their young — males, females, or both?
45. King Darius of Persia did it before de Lesseps. What?
46. In what country is the area referred-to in the old song, 'Roses are blooming in —'?
47. Spell the unpleasant word we pronounce as 'flem'.
48. What's the complementary angle of twenty degrees?
49. Luther Burbank became famous for breeding and developing many new varieties of — what?
50. What was a 'sennight'?

QUIZ 12
1. Who belongs in a ship's brig?
2. Which is the larger city — San Francisco or Los Angeles?
3. What was Lloyd George's first name?
4. What's meant by 'Greek calends (or kalends)'?
5. What's a collation, dietarily speaking?
6. Is Hansen's disease (leprosy) extremely, quite, or mildly contagious?
7. What's a Windsor knot?
8. Are the Rocky Mountains all within Canada?
9. Who is not allowed to enter the House of Commons?
10. How many different chemical elements are vital to the growth of plants — about 10, about 20, or over 30?

11. Is the Earth's distance from the Sun constant?
12. Five seconds. How many inches in a fathom?
13. Where did the chewing of 'gum' (chicle) originate?
14. When planting pieces of potato, one must see to it that each piece has one or more — what?
15. The various special types of curve obtained by slicing through a right circular cone are collectively called — what?
16. What's a manatee?
17. Is Sauterne a white or a red wine?
18. Do wasps and bees ever fight each other?
19. What's the difference between today's dragon-flies and those of prehistoric times?
20. What are the three elements of which alcohol is composed?
21. Who indulge in sibling rivalry?
22. The plural of bacillus?
23. What's the German name for Aix-la-Chapelle?
24. In what country did the discovery of radium occur?
25. What was the 'nationality' of Edward the Confessor's mother?
26. When the outer coating has been removed from rice, what's left?
27. To an Australian, is a billabong a tramp, his knapsack, or a backwater?
28. Why are fruit that don't grow on pine trees called pineapples?
29. A Mongolian people in Siberia gave their name to what handsome white Arctic breed of dog?
30. Bonnet and boot are what to an American motorist?
31. What do many male Buddhists deliberately become on a temporary basis?
32. What's the monetary unit of Holland — the Dutch mark?
33. Who composed 'Madame Butterfly'?
34. Is a loris an animal, a vegetable, a vehicle, or a type of eyeglass?
35. What Englishman invented printing from moveable type?
36. Of what is umber a shade?
37. In two words, how and from what is brandy made?
38. What are maracas?
39. After whom were towns (now a city) at the Atlantic end of the Panama Canal named?
40. Which is the earliest site of human settlement, among these — Cairo, Jerusalem, or Jericho?
41. Are there any glaciers in tropical regions?

42. From the name of what animal is the word 'muscle' derived?
43. Is coal ever mined from under the sea?
44. Of what is mycology the study?
45. In which century did the Synod of Whitby occur — 7th, 11th, or 14th?
46. In less then eight words, what would you be offered by a Mexican handing you a dish of frijoles?
47. What colour are the eggs of most species of bats?
48. What do we usually call the well-known Greek Island of Kérkira?
49. Who was prime minister at the time of Edward VIII's abdication?
50. Where would one find legless alewives?

QUIZ 13

1. Cheerful thought. About how many miles (laid end to end) would your blood-vessels total in length — 73; 730; 7300; 73,000? (Adult)
2. Where is it that 'Hope springs eternal'?
3. Who had a lady-friend with a highly oleaginous cognomen?
4. After Rome fell, wheeled vehicles became quite scarce in Europe. Why?
5. It's wise not to take a cold shower within two hours of doing what?
6. Americans remember Stratford-on-Avon for whom besides the Shakespeare family?
7. The biceps we usually refer to are in the upper arm What about the triceps?
8. Is a cairngorm a dagger, a semi-precious stone, or a monument of piled up rocks?
9. The mass migration northward of discontented Boers (1835-7) was called the 'Great — what'?
10. What plant, common in many rocky areas, is actually two different plant organisms living symbiotically?
11. What have the Sahara and the Dogger Bank in common?
12. Why are sombrero hats so called?
13. Partaking solely of which single substance, could one expect to survive the longest?
14. What seeds, used for flavouring, most nearly resemble those of caraway?
15. What's the word for 'gassiness' in the alimentary canal?
16. Do people (not necessarily in desperation) eat grasshoppers?

24

17. What gave us the word 'meander'?
18. How do mendicants make their living?
19. Give two names for structures (not of mud or stone) dwelt in by North American Indians.
20. Do adult dragonflies bite or sting people?
21. In one word, the main concern of demographers is the amount and distribution of — what?
22. Japan's an archipelago; and Tokyo's on its largest island, called — What?
23. Who was the first Russian ruler to have himself proclaimed Tsar?
24. Periodically, there has been trouble in regard to Amoy. What's Amoy?
25. Guam is a territory administered by what nation?
26. From what plant material, besides seeds, sap, and fruits, is alcohol most commonly made?
27. A plane figure bounded by four straight lines, regardless of its angles, is called a — what?
28. Do any butterflies migrate?
29. What planet was once named Herschel for its discoverer, and 'The Georgian' *by* its discoverer?
30. What shade of blue is favoured by most artists, realistically to depict a fine-weather daytime sky?
31. Newham College is for whom, and where? (Full answer.)
32. Into what is Australia divided?
33. Is North America's highest mountain in Canada, Alaska, or the rest of the US?
34. By what more imposing name do we know Edmond Dantes?
35. When is a clock simultaneously fast and slow?
36. What Italian city gave its name to a coin still circulating in Britain?
37. For what is Limoges particularly noted — cheese, perfume or china?
38. What British Crown Colony is at the mouth of the Canton River?
39. Who preceded Queen Juliana on the throne of Holland?
40. What's a nosegay?
41. What do peregrinators do?
42. Hydro-electric. Why 'hydro'?
43. Twelve soldiers stand in a line side by side. A rank? Or a file?
44. Who would be most concerned with his embouchure — an architect, a rifleman, or a trumpeter?

45. What's a punkah?
46. People who 'bleed easily', and among whom such bleeding is dangerously difficult to arrest, suffer from — what?
47. Complete this late film star's name: Sir Cedric — ?
48. What country is immediately south of Egypt, and is it larger or smaller in area than Egypt? (Full answer.)
49. The property of absorbing atmospheric moisture and dissolving in it is called — what?
50. Which is NOT an insect — scorpion, mantis, mite, weevil?

QUIZ 14

1. What tree is widely threatened by 'Dutch — disease'?
2. Put these in correct order, reading from west to east — Libya, Tunisia, Egypt, Algeria.
3. What's the popular definition of a 'straight line'?
4. Work in connection with what disease made Australia's Sister Kenney famous?
5. What country lies on the slope of Mount Titano?
6. What's a 'faux pas'?
7. Can a boxer's fist travel at faster than 100 mph in delivering a punch in the ring?
8. Who wrote 'Mrs Warren's Profession'?
9. For what is Lucullus remembered?
10. Does any species of bird fly higher than two miles up?
11. A postage stamp issued in Great Britain during whose reign is now the most valuable?
12. Where did the Carthaginians come from?
13. What 'vitamin' is really a complex of various vitamins?
14. Who wrote the line 'God of our fathers, known of old'?
15. What's a little unusual about the Russian vehicle called a troika?
16. What, in a few words, causes the seasons?
17. Did oranges originally come from Africa, Asia, or America?
18. Which is the greater distance — 2½ miles or 24 furlongs?
19. What are the two dots (as in 'Aïda') called, and what, in English, do they signify? (Full answer.)
20. What's the popular word for the long feathers on the necks of certain domesticated birds?
21. What's the highest mountain in Turkey?
22. What, predominantly, is the metallic element present in rubies?
23. Is the Yukon Territory part of Alaska, or part of British Columbia?

24. Correct this statement: 'George Washington's son ran twice for the office of President, but failed both times.'
25. Who is the present prime minister of Lapland?
26. What, frequently used by accountants, originated in India, being introduced into Europe by the Arabs?
27. Less colloquially, what's the shinbone called?
28. What, in the biblical phrase, is man's allotted span of life?
29. A better-known name for a tarboosh?
30. Which island both experienced nuclear testing and gave its name to a once startling item of beach wear?
31. Which two American states were named after Charles I?
32. What's meant by 'Q.E.D.'?
33. What's the square root of a quarter?
34. What ungainly creature, when excited, is said to 'sweat' blood?
35. What, notably, does the USA keep at Fort Knox?
36. Do finches have beaks like those of sparrows or those of blackbirds?
37. Writing, or playing, music in a different key is called — what?
38. A Mr Pratt gained added fame in the rôle of a monster, acting under what name?
39. In the place of worship used by persons of what faith was 'the holy of holies'?
40. What's a Blenheim Orange?
41. If flora is plant life, what's the corresponding word for animal life?
42. In two words, what, literally, does 'flotilla' mean?
43. Who wrote, in his own language, that 'All Gaul is divided into four parts'?
44. What's the latitude of the North Pole?
45. On the cubes in dice games, how many spots on the side opposite the 'five'?
46. Extermination of a whole population, tribe, or 'race' is referred-to in one word as — what?
47. In what country was (Andrew) Bonar Law, the British Conservative Prime Minister in 1922-3, born?
48. Lili — who? — was the subject of a German song that Allied troops adopted.
49. Was George Bernard Shaw born in England, Scotland, Ireland, or Wales?
50. Mr Pindling became Prime Minister of — what?

QUIZ 15

1. What's a blunderbuss?
2. Which of the United States still has the British Union Jack in its official flag?
3. In Egypt, notably, what meteorological phenomenon is called a khamsin?
4. How can one tell whether one has severed an artery?
5. What's the word for ambiguous speech; talking with a double meaning?
6. How do Newfoundlanders pronounce the name of their province?
7. Gold can be drawn out into an extremely fine wire. What, specifically, is this property called?
8. Did Thomas Mann ever receive a Nobel prize, and — if so — for what?
9. What is the central part of our planet believed to consist of?
10. Was Benjamin Franklin actually born in Boston, England or Boston, Massachusetts?
11. Where should one go in Australia to find zebras?
12. In what language did Sir Francis Bacon write most of his philosophical works?
13. Which borders on Mexico — Guatemala or Nicaragua?
14. Of what country (mainly) is the Yucatan peninsula a part?
15. What, besides a plant, is called plumbago?
16. From what substance in cows' milk can an excellent glue be made?
17. What important discovery do we owe to Doctors Banting and Best?
18. Meteors approaching Earth often burn up on the way. How about those approaching the Moon?
19. How much faster than ostriches can cassowaries fly?
20. On which side of a cow, normally, would she expect you to sit, in order to milk her by hand?
21. What do we call 12½ per cent of a gallon?
22. The name of what important substance means, literally, 'rock oil'?
23. Which Canadian province was named after a part of Great Britain?
24. What is Tabasco, culinarily speaking?
25. Where is Ghent?
26. Distinguish between a tarpon and a tarpaulin.
27. What famous man had a father called Pepin the Short?

28

28. What's a cockade?
29. In the interior of Canada, is the winter-summer temperature range as much as 120 degrees F., 145, 170?
30. What's the common word for a colour, that of unbleached undyed wool?
31. Is the population of Africa more or less than 200 million?
32. What's the difference, if any, between a sinecure and a pedicure?
33. What do we call crosses shaped like the cross of the Order of St John?
34. What does 'trove', in 'treasure trove', mean?
35. What, notably, did the incredible Norwegian, Mensen Ernst, do?
36. Where would a soldier wear a shako?
37. What's the popular name given to the beard-like plant growths that hang from tree branches in semi-tropical areas?
38. What's a claymore?
39. Which is not a human blood-type — A, B, A-B, O, O-H?
40. What's a grampus?
41. Ferdinand and Isabella. How were they related 'by blood'?
42. Another name for Taurus?
43. Where should the word 'I' appear on a formal invitation?
44. What's the capital of Hong Kong?
45. As a rule, what colour of flower has the strongest perfume?
46. Are garrulous individuals quarrelsome, nervous, or talkative?
47. What enables an owl to fly so silently?
48. Is a polyglot a multilingual person, a crowd, or a glutton?
49. A certain clock strikes a single chime, and on the hour only. If it takes 5 seconds to strike five o'clock, how long does it take to strike ten?
50. What's a peccadillo?

QUIZ 16

1. Which land animals have the most ribs?
2. Who (in 1798) warned, if rather exaggeratedly, of the coming population problem'?
3. From what sedge did the early Egyptians make writing material?
4. 'Corps': (a) how pronounced, (b) what's its plural form? (Full answer.)
5. What 'quoth the raven'?
6. Whose followers wore *red* shirts?

7. Which city is referred to in a hymn as 'blessed with milk and honey'?

8. What is vichyssoise?

9. 'Zloty' means 'golden'. What country applied the word to its monetary unit?

10. Yorkshire Pudding: flour, salt, milk, gravy fat. What ingredient is missing?

11. In all of today's alphabets, what's the oldest letter?

12. What are read, or published, to give notice of an intended marriage?

13. Kitchener, Ontario, was so re-named during World War I. Its previous name was — ?

14. Who, especially, lived in pueblos?

15. One of the world's greatest medical centres is in Rochester, Minnesota or Rochester, New York. Which city?

16. What's another name for the lime tree that doesn't provide citrus fruits?

17. Antarctica contains how much of the world's ice — 30 per cent, 60 per cent, or 90 per cent?

18. Of which vitamin, notably, are fresh ripe tomatoes an excellent source?

19. Which is the first animal listed in any good English dictionary?

20. Which wouldn't one use as a herb used to flavour food dishes — ramie, chervil, rosemary, hominy, basil?

21. Who has long been called the King of Swing?

22. Why can't rust burn?

23. Hair used to be horrendously tinted orange-red with henna. What did henna come from?

24. In the game of blackjack, what is the highest permissible 'score'?

25. Where is the word 'Maru' most frequently seen?

26. Is the hypotenuse of a triangle always its longest side?

27. To whom was the appellation 'Lion of Judah' given?

28. From what kind of camel is mohair obtained?

29. Are sturgeon ever found in North American lakes or rivers?

30. What did competitors, in the original 'Olympic Games', wear?

31. Of what colour is ochre a shade?

32. What country (originally) was often referred-to as a sub-continent?

33. Would a man be embarrassed to show his lady friend his cicatrix?

34. One of the hottest spices has the 'coldest name.' What name?
35. Which herbs' names mean (a) 'wise', and (b) 'tasty'?
36. 'Anti-' means 'against'. What about 'ante-'?
37. What German word, meaning 'substitute', gained wide use in the forties?
38. The ordinary potato. Is it actually a stem or a root?
39. Natives of Sri Lanka aren't Senegalese, but — what?
40. A cramp in the intercostal muscles is 'popularly' known as — what?
41. What well-known instrument resembles a dulcimer, but is played by plucking?
42. Where is Keflavik airport?
43. What's the word for a coil of hair worn at the back of a woman's head?
44. With what do chickens 'chew' their food?
45. Did Rembrandt ever paint a portrait of himself?
46. What gave linoleum its name?
47. What's a salver?
48. Name the birthplace of Joan of Arc.
49. What event did the authors Nordhoff and Hall collaboratively write about in great detail?
50. Would it be possible to cross a Chihuahua dog with a St Bernard?

QUIZ 17

1. What term is most frequently used for a North American Indian's baby?
2. What does 'bucolic' mean?
3. Whom did Disraeli characterise as 'a sophisticated rhetorician inebriated with the exuberance of his own verbosity'?
4. What country, a small fraction of Africa in size, has a coastline almost as long?
5. Where does the water go at low tide?
6. What are your pleura? (Hint: pleurisy.)
7. Which King Louis was guillotined?
8. What fine hard white (or mottled) soap is made with olive oil and soda?
9. Are mango trees usually found growing in swamps?
10. What does a whiting have in common with whitebait?
11. What would you have if you cooked ocarinas in olive oil?
12. For what surprisingly accurate computation is Eratosthenes best remembered?

13. Who was the father of Queen Victoria?
14. What is feldspar?
15. On what island are Hobart and Launceston?
16. How do archer-fish 'catch' the flying insects they like to eat?
17. Who. in what's now the USA., were called Redcoats?
18. What's 'Danish Blue'?
19. Name the two well-known types of cephalopod creatures.
20. At the commencement of a game of chess, how many pawns on the board?
21. Is it true that Charles Dickens died disappointed at never having visited the United States?
22. If a coracle is a small primitive boat, what's a carapace?
23. Is the pronoun 'everyone' singular or plural?
24. Is a square a rectangle?
25. What are lenticels?
26. Was that a spinster who 'lived in a shoe'?
27. Two names are coupled with Gilbert. One's Sullivan. What's 'tother?
28. What talent first won Frederick Austerlitz his fame, under another name?
29. To what objective did 'The Trail of '98' lead?
30. How many letters of the alphabet stand for musical notes?
31. In what year was China's last Imperial ruler overthrown — 1882, 1911, or 1936?
32. Are the odds high or low that there is snow or ice on Mars?
33. What do poets mean by 'ebon'?
34. Of what plant is 'aniseed' the fruit?
35. The average full head of blond hair consists of about 140,000; 400,000; or 750,000 hairs. How many?
36. Who painted 'The Boyhood of Raleigh'?
37. Whom did Nicodemus help to bury?
38. After whom or what was the landau (and landaulet) named?
39. Name the TWO plant emblems of Wales. And its animal emblem. (All or nothing.)
40. What extraordinary feat was accomplished by Dr J. Piccard and Lt. D. Walsh in a bathyscaphe (the Trieste)?
41. Who — not King Cole — was dubbed ('The Merry Monarch'?
42. What 'Baron', hero of a book by Rudolf Raspe, related highly extravagant tales of his own prowess?
43. The word for animals that eat both plant and animal substances?

44. What's the square root of 289?
45. What do we mean by 'a person in his nonage'?
46. Apparent change in frequency, or pitch, of sound produced by something approaching or receding at high speed is called the — (what) effect?
47. The origin of 'goodbye'?
48. Was Napoleon the first, second, or third husband of his first wife?
49. What molluscs are most often found attached to ships' hulls?
50. What does the dove, as a symbol of peace, carry?

QUIZ 18
1. With what nuts is the name 'Jordan' most associated?
2. What letter, more than any other, starts the names of national capitals?
3. Which black heavyweight boxer won the world championship in Sydney, and lost it in Havana?
4. Name two U.S. presidents who had 'oo' in their names.
5. Apart from cooks and housewives, who stuffs animals?
6. How do Bermudans normally get their drinking water — from a lake, by distilling sea-water, collecting rainwater, or Artesian wells?
7. The author, please, of 'Rebecca'?
8. For what purpose is a woomera used, in Australia?
9. In what city was the first-recorded game of ice hockey played?
10. If one could get over revulsion at the idea, would one find rattlesnake-meat good to eat?
11. Alone, in a wagon-lit, what would you expect to do?
12. What did the finding of 'The Piltdown Man' prove?
13. Whose wife was the reputedly shrewish Xanthippe?
14. What kind of weather is usually associated with 'the dog days'?
15. What French word have we borrowed to apply to a procession — especially that involved with a funeral?
16. Who was the father of James I of England?
17. How much less does a hundredweight weigh in North America than in Britain?
18. Which country, continuingly, is Britain's oldest ally?
19. To what people does the term 'Romany' apply?
20. What's rather unusual about true hermaphrodites?
21. What does ESP stand for?
22. What do dermatologists do?

24. What kind of substance is used to etch designs into a copper plate?

24. Which normally weighs more — the white or the yolk of an egg?

25. What's the derivation of the world 'vaccinate' — a cow, a needle, blood, or protection?

26. How many 'L's' in the Yugoslav spelling of what we call Belgrade?

27. Is Copenhagen on an island, or on the mainland, of Denmark?

28. Which is longer, the Suez Canal or the Panama Canal?

29. What, to the nearest whole pound per square inch, is the atmospheric pressure at sea level?

30. By what symbol and name was the 'Mafia' once known?

31. What island near San Francisco was, for a long time, the site of a maximum-security prison?

32. Who, for some years, has been South Africa's most successful (and appropriately named) professional golfer?

33. What bird gave its name to the word 'pedigree'? (tricky)!

34. To the 'Old Contemptibles', who was the best-known 'Mademoiselle'?

35. Do elephants have more or less teeth than people?

36. What country owns Elba?

37. Does food normally go down your sarcophagus or your trachea?

38. Forgetting about babies, what did farmers once use cradles for?

39. What's the name of the beautiful blue stone (containing sodium, aluminium, and sulphur) sometimes used as a pigment?

40. Ornithologists study birds. What was an ornithopter?

41. What word, in English dictionaries, is always spelled incorrectly?

42. If a man is knighted, what title does his wife bear?

43. What was the significance of the name Gemini, for one series of space flights?

44. What's the word for running along the surface, in the case of aeroplanes (or seaplanes)?

45. What's the colour of steam?

46. Is zoology a branch of biology, or vice versa?

47. What great river is frequently referred-to as 'Big Muddy'?

48. Marconi's first Transatlantic wireless signals were sent between Poldhu, Cornwall, and where?

49. What name is given the period of a disease, following infection, but prior to appearance of symptoms?

50. England was never ruled by a Richard IV — but who called himself that?

QUIZ 19

1. What whole country was named after a Briton?

2. Taking a pill, and then one every $1\frac{1}{2}$ hours, how long would 7 pills last you?

3. Was Plato a pupil of Socrates, or vice versa?

4. Proteins break down into compounds which we call — what?

5. What do we call papillae found in the mouth?

6. Which is the deadliest gas present in the exhaust from ordinary internal combustion engines?

7. Is Béchamel a rich white sauce, a fine red wine, or a card game?

8. Do gorillas spend most of their time, awake, on two feet or on all fours?

9. Which is the most serious — a first, second, or third degree burn?

10. What happens to a banana 'tree', as a rule, after its fruit has been removed?

11. What is a hakenkreuz?

12. Who was — to the ancient Romans — among other things, goddess of the Moon and patroness of virgins?

13. Where, in Britain, would one go to gather seakale?

14. Which European country claims to be ideologically closest to communist China?

15. How many queen bees, normally, are there in an average populated hive?

16. A gig is a light carriage — with how many wheels?

17. Do we owe the system of chemical symbols used today (e.g. H for hydrogen) to Linnaeus, Berzelius, or Copernicus?

18. Whom do we know for certain to have travelled overland to China, from Europe, before Marco Polo did it?

19. To which are eels more closely related — snakes or fish?

20. Who introduced paper-making into Europe?

21. Who went looking for 'The Fountain of Youth'?

22. Is the antonym of 'antonym' a homonym, pseudonym, or synonym?

23. When was the mountainous 'Far West' of the country known as *Upper* Canada?

24. What's meant by 'using the vernacular'?
25. On which vessel did Charles Darwin make his famous voyage into the Pacific Ocean?
26. 'Permissible' or 'permissable'?
27. Name two islands named for Christian festivals.
28. Reverse a word for a highly unpleasant odour, and get a word meaning 'unites intimately'.
29. What is flensing?
30. With what variety of acacia would most Australians be most familiar?
31. What's meant by 'Iceland spar' — a kind of rock, mast, or toffee?
32. Where are both cods' tongues and seal-flippers quite often eaten?
33. Mohammed Ahmed besieged General Gordon in Khartoum, and was widely referred to as 'The — what'?
34. Would you describe the odour of nitrogen as unpleasant, sweetish, or 'acid'?
35. The battle of Bosworth Field ended what conflict?
36. Whom did Bobby Fischer beat in the finals that won him the world's chess championship?
37. Whom, if anyone, did Adolf Hitler marry?
38. What was the original meaning of 'flagrant'?
39. Biblically, who was the world's first baby?
40. Which Canadian province has become the most important Canadian source of petroleum?
41. With what kind of song do you associate gondolas?
42. What's the acid in vinegar?
43. How were fruits usually dried in olden times?
44. Rehoboam succeeded his father as king of Israel. Who was his father?
45. In what game is the word 'stalemate' important?
46. Who is credited with writing the Iliad?
47. For what, notably, did Mafeking become famous?
48. Is there any connection between 'salami' and 'Salome' and 'salaam'?
49. At which end does a worm feed?
50. Who was called 'The Iron Chancellor'?

QUIZ 20

1. A variety of what kind of tree has the largest known seeds?
2. Verse 35 in chapter 2 of John is the Bible's shortest. How does it read?
3. Who was the tearful Iranian prime minister involved in the

expropriation of 'foreign-owned' oil companies some years ago?

4. By what name are the wars between Rome and Carthage known?
5. In a castle, who or what was a 'bailey'?
6. Of what island is Bridgetown the capital?
7. 'For men may come, and men may go, but — what'?
8. The word for a metal cap like that at the bottom end of an umbrella?
9. Famous surnames, all ornithological — (a) nurse, (b) architect, (c) sailor. (Full answer.)
10. If a man spends two-thirds of his money, and then 40 per cent of what he had left, leaving him £6, what did he start with?
11. From what country do we get Drambuie liqueur?
12. Who 'discovered' oxygen?
13. Where is the city of Hilo?
14. London, Ontario, is on what river?
15. What country is the major supplier of true sable furs?
16. Are any bacteria beneficial to mankind?
17. Did Edmund Spenser devote 20 weeks, months, or years to writing his 'Faerie Queen'?
18. Is gorgonzola cheese named after its inventor, a place, or tiny edible cheese-mites?
19. How is the French word for 'onion' spelled?
20. What is the great whirlpool south of the Lofoten Is. called?
21. What country today has within it the site of ancient Babylon?
22. Are Atlantic and Pacific salmon the same creatures?
23. What (tiny) kind of insect serves as a pollinator of figs?
24. What nickname was commonly applied to the pirate 'skull and crossbones' flag?
25. Is a tuba a 'brass' or a 'woodwind'?
26. What insect is the most familiar example of the order Hymenoptera?
27. Do Russians make tea in, wear, eat, or ride in, a droshky?
28. What's three times the half of a half of a half?
29. What's the best thing (so far) to apply immediately to a bee-sting?
30. What's the most plentiful solid element in the Earth's crust?
31. Correctly pronounce 'verbatim'.
32. Typhus is caused by a Rickettsia, a minute body apparently intermediate between — what, and what?

33. What letter starts the first row of letters on a standard English typewriter keyboard?
34. Name four consonants that, simply lettered, look the same upside down.
35. The name of what mineral quite inappropriately means 'inextinguishable'?
36. What kind of person is doleful?
37. In what county was the great Captain Cook born?
38. Of what substance do one's nails and hair mainly consist — keratin, chitin, or chyle?
39. Who painted the 'Mona Lisa'?
40. Emmer and einkorn were wild forms of what?
41. What's a substance called that facilitates a chemical reaction by its presence, while itself remaining unchanged?
42. Correctly pronounce 'wary'.
43. What famous document began — 'When in the course of human events it becomes necessary . . . ?'
44. What's the shape of the horizon?
45. The word for an orchestra conductor's wand?
46. Do newts go through a 'tadpole' stage, like frogs?
47. Cabriolets were one-horse carriages. What were cabrioles?
48. How many sons did Johann Sebastian Bach have — two, five, or eleven?
49. Who get more ulcers, men or women?
50. What's the capital city of British Columbia?

QUIZ 21
1. A strange and expensive substance used in perfumery comes from the sperm whale. What is it called?
2. Who is said to have stolen fire from heaven?
3. On what would one find metal rowels?
4. What kind of school-book is named for an individual who never existed?
5. What Hebrew word do we use for a 'test word', or identifying catchword?
6. For what was the goose-step originally a test?
7. Which has the greater area — all of Ireland or all of Iceland?
8. Who, in prison, compiled the famous 'Morte d'Arthur'?
9. How many times was Camembert Premier of France?
10. What's carrageen, and what kind of substance do we get from it?
11. Was Greece ever part of the Roman Empire?

12. What mainland area is closest to St Helena? ('Africa' not specific enough.)
13. If a Latin document were found, its author stating that he 'visited Britain in 55 BC', how would you know it to be false?
14. What do South Africans call their grassy 'prairie' land?
15. What queen took poison after finally being defeated by Seutonius Paulinus?
16. What do cucumbers and grapes have in common, as edible plant fruits; with each other, but not with apples?
17. Apart from being a 'frame' for a skirt, what's a pannier?
18. By whom was the last Doge of Venice deposed?
19. What did the Assyrians do with inflated pigskins?
20. Was St Patrick born in Ireland?
21. Normally, how long does food remain in the human stomach — about four hours; eight; twelve?
22. What happened to Rome when Tarquinius Superbus was deposed?
23. If this is spelled incorrectly, correct it: sphagetti.
24. What adjective does a doctor use for 'pertaining to the womb'?
25. What's the word for charging an unconscionably high rate of interest?
26. What word is most commonly applied to the American Indian's 'shell money'?
27. 'Mosquito' means 'little fly'. Flies and mosquitos belong to the order Diptera. What does 'Diptera' literally mean?
28. Wild ducks love it, but is *wild* rice used as food by people?
29. Flowering plants of what popular genus are called flags?
30. What gave the whippoorwill its name?
31. What does 'pinxit' mean, after a name?
32. Wrote Southey — 'But 'twas a famous victory.' What was?
33. What famous man is said to have swum ashore from a shipwreck, a sword between his teeth, and documents in one hand?
34. What large thistle provides delectable eating?
35. Of what country is Managua the capital?
36. Which sense is best served by the tip of the tongue?
37. Kidnapping an insensible man for enforced service as a sailor was called what? (British *or* American term will do).
38. What is the primary function of carbohydrates in our diet?
39. Are any clouds (in the sky) actually solid?
40. Of what element is spinach a particularly good food source?

41. What's the term applied to any substance that evaporates rapidly at ordinary temperatures?
42. What's kept in a bittern?
43. What's meant by 'antipasto'?
44. What — outside the Commonwealth — calls itself 'The Old Dominion'?
45. Cryptogams are blossomless plants. Add 'r', and you get a word meaning — what?
46. How many 'r's' in the name of the second month?
47. Species of what kind of vertebrate creature frequently spend the winter frozen within solid ice, and survive?
48. What part of a kangaroo is favoured for making soup?
49. What's a cockchafer?
50. Is the Irrawaddy river entirely within Burma?

QUIZ 22
1. Which sport is attended by the greatest total number of people in the USA?
2. Who changed history by defeating the Danes near Edington (Ethandune)?
3. Are 'tidal waves' ever over 100 feet in height?
4. Is the Earth's crust generally thicker or thinner under the ocean than under land surfaces?
5. Where, and by what, are young sea-horses raised?
6. Identify Charlotte Russe.
7. What were named Volapuk and Ido?
8. What's a merganser?
9. What proof have we that some mountain-sides were once ocean-bottoms?
10. The antonym of 'deny'?
11. Who, in their dancing, swing 'poi balls' in unison?
12. Women need more of what metallic element in their diet than do men?
13. Before telephonic cables were laid, how were Transatlantic telephone conversations transmitted?
14. Devotees used to throw themselves under the wheels bearing an enormous statue of Krishna, referred to as — what?
15. What do these electrical terms have in common — ampere, ohm, volt, farad, galvanism, joule?
16. In Canada what body, parliamentarily at least, most nearly correspond to the House of Lords?
17. To what order of insects do butterflies and moths belong?
18. Where is the Earth's longest mountain range?
19. Does anything dissolve in mercury?

20. Do the male or the female mosquitoes sting you?
21. 'Marry in haste, — — —'?
22. What do stage and TV people call the various objects used to dress up a 'set', or to be handled or moved by the performers. (Not including musical instruments.)
23. In what famous work is Captain Hook a character?
24. A senatorial election is for the position of senator. What kind is for that of governor?
25. What's the device used for 'tracing', or rather copying, a plan or drawing to a different scale?
26. What's the key ingredient in chow mein?
27. The Hudson's Bay Company was chartered by Charles II, primarily to procure what?
28. What, normally, is the hardest substance in a healthy human body?
29. What was the reputed occupation of Aesop, the teller of fables?
30. Who succeeded Harold Macmillan as Prime Minister?
31. What's the general term applied to insects of the order 'Coleoptera'?
32. If anthracite is 'hard' coal, what term is generally applied to 'soft' coal?
33. What celestial body is involved with setting the date of Easter Sunday?
34. Is Lake Michigan entirely within the USA, within Canada, or partly within each?
35. What religious symbolism does the shamrock sometimes serve?
36. In what opera does a Japanese maiden fall in love with an American naval officer?
37. Is you had angina pectoris, where should you take it?
38. Reverse a word meaning 'reel', into a word for 'knitting stitches'.
39. What semi-precious stone's name ends the way zircon starts?
40. Which is larger in area — France or the province of Québec?
41. What, besides a pack of cards and a surface to play upon, is indispensable for the playing of cribbage by two people?
42. Three Edwards (I, II, III) reigned in succession. Who were the next three kings in succession to use the same name?
43. For what is Captain Frederick Marryat best remembered?
44. Calendar, colander, calender. Which one glazes paper or cloth?

45. When did the United Nations take over administration of the Panama Canal zone?
46. Is 'polysyllabic' that?
47. What popular French phrase is applied to a private little chat between two persons?
48. To be a paragon, what must weigh 100 carats or more?
49. Spell the word for an ancient Egyptian ruler, pronounced 'faro'.
50. Who reigned, in Great Britain, immediately following the death of William II?

QUIZ 23

1. What kind of headache got its name from words meaning 'half of the skull'?
2. What would an American Indian do with a calumet?
3. Which was there first — St Paul's Cathedral, the Monument, or the Tower of London?
4. What, pharmaceutically, is A.S.A.?
5. How far below sea level is the shore of the Dead Sea? Nearly 900, nearly 1,300, or nearly 2,200 feet?
6. Where do many Slavic women wear babushkas?
7. 'Myriad' refers to a specific number. What?
8. The abalone has a beautifully iridescent shell. What's done with its broad 'foot'?
9. Who were Eng and Chang?
10. The Taj Mahal's main (tomb) building is built of what stone?
11. What's a year called that equals the time in which the Earth makes a single complete revolution around the Sun?
12. What do the Dutch call the land areas reclaimed from the Zuider Zee?
13. Did Zeppelins manage to drop any bombs on London during World War I?
14. Whence did Pheidippides run from to Athens?
15. Why were buttons put on men's sleeves (by Frederick the Great)?
16. What do gregarious people like?
17. What's the short, narrow, little, one-hand-operated 'spade', used by gardeners, called?
18. Suicide, in the U.K., is punishable by a prison term of how many years?
19. What four-legged creatures like to wash their food before eating it?

20. What cloth is supposed to have been worn by the men of the Sherwood Forest? (Two words).
21. 'I think that I shall never see, a poem — — — —'?
22. In one word, what kind of son is a prodigal one?
23. In the stomach of what kind of creature is Jonah said to have spent a rather unpleasant 72 hours?
24. What's the name commonly given to a measurement of approximately 2.54 centimetres?
25. Which is usually the greater, net weight or gross weight?
26. The Peloponnesus (—os) is a major peninsula of what country?
27. Human mothers average in weight about twenty times that of their babies. How about kangaroos? 11, 20, 90, or 2,100?
28. Why is the word 'atom' inappropriate?
29. When new wine was ready to drink, they used to advertise it by hanging a bush over the door — hence what saying?
30. What made Louis Washkansky famous?
31. What's semolina made from?
32. Has Halley's Comet been seen from Earth on more or less than 20 occasions since the birth of Christ?
33. Which, to Roman Catholics, are the more serious — mortal sins or venial sins?
34. What suggested Venezuela's name?
35. Collectively, and in English, what are members of the pea and bean family called?
36. To a gourmet — depending on where he is — what would York and Virginia suggest?
37. How many more letters in the longest name of a month than in the shortest?
38. Were the dinosaurs warm-blooded, or cold-blooded creatures?
39. What's the metallic element present in lime?
40. Immense humanoid creatures, resembling the 'Abominable Snowman' of the Himalayas, have been reported seen: where else?
41. Mussulmans do what?
42. Of what would you build a corduroy road?
43. What medicinal substance comes from a 'bean' that isn't?
44. For how many years was Catherine the Great empress of Austria?
45. From what country came the steel for the famous Sydney Harbour Bridge?
46. What made Helen Wills (Moody) famous?
47. What are persimmons?

48. What name is given to dried muscadine grapes?

49. Was Troy weight used in ancient Asia Minor?

50. What was the one-word name often used for China, in earlier times?

QUIZ 24

1. Why do Eskimos these days never take to the water in kulaks?

2. By far the greatest proportion by weight of matter in the universe consists of what element?

3. Medellin is rarely in the news. Yet it is a very large (and very beautiful) city. In what country?

4. What immigrant boy amassed an enormous fortune and devoted much of it to libraries?

5. In what field of activity did Selma Lagerlöf earn her Nobel prize?

6. Name the famous canal leading from Inverness to Fort William.

7. Musk, used in perfumery, is obtained from — what?

8. What, literally, is meant by 'tandem'?

9. What are viviparous creatures?

10. What is 'next to godliness'?

11. What, notably, did Wilhelm Konrad von Röntgen discover?

12. From what kind of plant is saffron obtained?

13. How many 'U's' in the word for a native of Portugal?

14. When one cube stands squarely on another of identical size, how many square sides are left exposed?

15. What is the essential element in the evolutionary principle of 'natural selection'?

16. What disease is known to be spread by crickets?

17. Name the submarine featured in 'Twenty Thousand Leagues under the Sea'.

18. What was the relationship between Charles and Mary Lamb?

19. 'Age cannot wither her' — whom?

20. In what country are the mouths of the Rhine and Rhône respectively? (Both needed.)

21. What kind of tail does a beaver have — rat-like, paddle-like, or curled up?

22. What's a peccary?

23. What sound in English is spelled in the greatest number of different ways?

24. What's a quandary?

25. Members of what bird family (actually, order) sometimes spread the highly unpleasant disease, psittacosis, among humans?
26. What's the word for a young male horse sired by a gelding?
27. Why 'hypo' in 'hypodermic'?
28. How many well-known writers were named Alexandre Dumas?
29. What piece of furniture gave cathedrals that name?
30. Where is Mount Logan?
31. What causes kwashiorkor among deprived people, especially in the tropics?
32. Is the retina in the front or the back of the eye, or roughly half-way between them?
33. How many times did Christopher Columbus land on the coast of China?
34. What's another name for Lake Geneva? (Not beginning with 'G'.)
35. The butler didn't do it — but what did sutlers do?
36. What county is most frequently called 'The Garden of England'?
37. Who was Tenzing Norkhay?
38. What's another one-word name for the island of Taiwan?
39. Which highly contagious disease, now relatively rare in Europe, used to kill a half million or more people a year there?
40. Answer completely. Give two words, in one of which the letter 'U', and in the other the letter 'O', are respectively pronounced as though each were a letter 'I'.
41. What would one do with a microtome?
42. What vehicle had a 'money' name?
43. What's a maxixe?
44. Who are world-famous as the ' — Globetrotters'?
45. Name the immense plain along the central south coast of Australia.
46. Who or what was Montenegro?
47. Which is the better conductor of electricity — tap water or pure distilled water?
48. Was Columbus born in Spain, Portugal, Malta, or Italy?
49. What unusual food was supplied 'from heaven' to the Israelites in the wilderness?
50. What Florentine's name is often applied to scheming unscrupulousness in political activity?

QUIZ 25

1. Would it be possible for one cow to yield 4,000 gallons of milk in one year?
2. Whose life was the subject of 'The Agony and the Ecstasy'?
3. Who use maulsticks (mahlsticks) for support?
4. What's a 'tornado' at sea called?
5. What old Irish province comprised Waterford, Cork, Limerick, Clare, Tipperary, and Kerry?
6. How tall was the tallest man of whom we have any record? (Within 2 ins.)
7. What's pedagogy?
8. Before they became residences they were stables: before that, mews accommodated what creatures?
9. In what part of one's body is the cochlea?
10. What's the dark fine-grained rock massively present at great depths, and nearer the surface of much of the ocean floor?
11. What kind of alga (sea weed) often grows to hundreds of feet in length?
12. The coronation of what British sovereign, during the past 100 years, was postponed due to that sovereign's being ill?
13. Which has greater population — Mexico City or Montréal?
14. What name is usually applied to members of the Society of Friends?
15. Has Mount Fujiyama been known to erupt in the past 500 years?
16. Where would one normally place a lintel?
17. For what discovery is Dr William Harvey best remembered?
18. 'If you have tears, — — — — — '?
19. Where could you expect to be served a delectable sukiyaki?
20. What's one, of a pair, of dice, called?
21. Which 'country' issues postage stamps — Monaco, Vatican State, Pitcairn Island?
22. Did both the famous Wright Brothers die before 1930?
23. To what practical use, in industry, have caged birds (usually canaries) been put?
24. How many 'numbers' (exclusive of zeros) are there on a regular roulette wheel?
25. The abbreviation usually used for 'barrels', please.
26. What's the more professional-sounding word for a 'rupture' (e.g. inguinal, umbilical)?
27. What deficiency-disease, notably, is due to a dietary lack of vitamin B_1?

28. What are the individual bones of one's 'backbone' called?
29. From what cape are American space-shots fired?
30. In what respect is the Panama Canal out-of-date?
31. Is Chinese traditionally read from left to right, right to left, or top to bottom?
32. Can you supply Field Marshal B. L. Montgomery's middle name?
33. What's the capital city of Bermuda?
34. What part — if any — of an ermine hasn't turned white for the winter?
35. What practice gave 'sabotage' its name?
36. What's the name commonly applied to the tree, frequently seen in the Indo-Pacific region, that — supported by dozens of trunks — may provide shade over a very large area?
37. Demeter was the Greek goddess of cereal crops. With what Roman goddess was she identified?
38. How is mica manufactured?
39. Little Miss Muffet got plenty of nourishment from curds, but did the whey have any nutritional value at all?
40. Which, in feet, is nearest to representing the height of Mont Blanc — 13,669; 15,781; 17,224?
41. Where, in Ontario, Canada, are major Shakespearian Festivals held?
42. Which was not part of French Indo-China — North Vietnam, Thailand, Annam, Cambodia, Laos?
43. Does one normally produce more or less than a pint of saliva a day?
44. Distinguish between MANSARD and HANSARD.
45. What do ice-hockey players knock about, besides each other?
46. From what type of tree is sago obtained?
47. Who is best remembered as a leader of the infamous Spanish Inquisition?
48. To get some trepanning done, would you properly go to a forester, a surgeon, a chef, or a gold prospector?
49. There are incisors on one side of a canine tooth: what, next to the canine, on the other side?
50. What's a salvo, to a sailor?

QUIZ 26
1. Three seconds: how many white keys BETWEEN 'C' and the next 'C', on a piano?
2. What food substance does the cotton plant provide?

3. Who was the first *English* duke? What dukedom? (Full answer.)
4. Which is closer to the Sun — the Earth or the Moon?
5. What was 'Sphairistike'?
6. What's the smallest true bone in the human body?
7. What substance is indigo?
8. What were sesterces?
9. 'Filly' is to 'mare' as what is to 'cow'?
10. What's the word for a short, light, opera?
11. What, specifically, do agnostics deny?
12. What is meant by 'legal tender'?
13. Which is greater — the length of the island of New Guinea, or the distance from London to Moscow?
14. How were diamonds formed in the earth?
15. Who wrote both 'Scaramouche' and 'Captain Blood'?
16. The Treaty of Versailles followed what war?
17. What's a tocsin?
18. Is bullfighting now illegal in Mexico?
19. By what name is François Marie Arouet better remembered?
20. What is measured from the year we call 622 AD?
21. An impulsive stealer is a kleptomaniac: a highly impulsive drinker, a — what?
22. Among the three of them, how many sides do a pentagon, a heptagon, and an octagon have?
23. Which is most concerned with early artifacts of Man — an archaeologist, a palaeontologist, or an archivist?
24. In earlier times, men referred to earth, air, fire, and water as the four elements. Which of these is actually an element?
25. What fragrance does that of verbena (in soap, for example) resemble?
26. What drug was named for the god of dreams?
27. Who played the part of the energetic Mr Fogg in Mike Todd's 'Around the World in Eighty Days'?
28. Schnapps. Eaten or drunk?
29. What's the word for the minimum number present required to make a meeting 'official'?
30. Where, if you'll excuse me, are your leucocytes?
31. In which state is it a custom to give some prominent men the purely honorary 'title' of 'colonel'? Virginia, Tennessee, Texas, or Kentucky?
32. Who is usually credited with remarking that 'an army marches on its stomach'?
33. What's the correct plural form of the word 'enigma'?

34. Which is more nearly circular in cross-section — curly hair or straight hair?

35. Where has the condor multiplied to the point where it is hunted down as a pest?

36. Where are Godthaab, Frederikshaab, and Julianehaab?

37. Which, notably, is Portugal's port port?

38. What's the highest mountain in Greece?

39. Apart from sugar, what's the main ingredient, specifically, of meringue?

40. In one word what's a pergola?

41. Does the name Cox suggest strawberries, grapes, or apples?

42. Who was nicknamed 'the wisest fool in Christendom'?

43. What's the best-known example of the genus Ilex?

44. Is most of Greece a flat plain or mountainous?

45. What's a weimaraner?

46. Does sound travel fastest through water, through air, or through a vacuum?

47. Who created the character Hiawatha — Longfellow, Tennyson, or James Fenimore Cooper?

48. What word, beginning with H, applies both to an evergreen tree and a poisonous umbelliferous plant. (Socrates would know it.)

49. What's the name for a bottle holding two quarts of, say, champagne?

50. What's the gas that bubbles up in bottled effervescent beverages?

QUIZ 27

1. What common metal burns brightest?

2. A Louis XIV drillmaster gave his name to ultra-strict military disciplinarians. What name?

3. What do the Germans call a 'wald'?

4. How many two-inch cubes make a twenty-inch cube?

5. Why are penknives so called?

6. What famous bridge, near Bristol, do we owe to the engineer Isambard K. Brunel?

7. Distinguish between (a) procrastination, and (b) prevarication.

8. Correct this. 'Who do you want to see?'

9. The name of what great Canadian city means 'meeting place'?

10. What cheese is best for grating over onion soup (and certain others)?

11. In what country is Kandahar?

12. What was the full date of the first day of this century?
13. What, besides the Moon, plays a part in causing the tides?
14. Which country now produces the greatest tonnage of coffee 'beans'?
15. What does the motto 'Ich Dien' mean?
16. How many obtuse angles can a triangle have?
17. Papaya 'melons' are delicious. Do they grow on trees or vines?
18. Which would one prefer to smoke — a Haida, a hookah, a howdah, or a Hoosier?
19. What causes goitre, as a rule?
20. Who fathered twins and named them Hamnet and Judith?
21. Are there more or less 'Red Indians' than there were 150 years ago?
22. In what year did H. G. Wells write 'Dr Jekyll and Mr Hyde?
23. What, originally, was an equerry?
24. Give an ordinary everyday English word with six 'S's' in it.
25. What qualities do many Chinese ascribe to the powdered 'horns' of the rhinoceros?
26. What name is often applied to usually calm regions, at sea, between those where trade-winds blow?
27. Whom do misogynists detest?
28. What domestic animal's name is sometimes applied to a man's beard?
29. What, in particular, gives mulligatawny its distinctive flavour?
30. What's kept under the seat of the Coronation Chair?
31. Can sugar be commercially obtained from trees?
32. What does 'non compos mentis' mean?
33. Does about one in 100, in 500, in 1000, or in 5000 of the world's population presently understand Esperanto?
34. How soon after Rudolf Hess landed in Scotland, during World War II, was he shot as a spy?
35. Where is most of the world's iodine mined?
36. What happens to an opossum when it's frightened?
37. What kind of fish, mainly, do Portuguese fishermen catch in castanets?
38. Is the circumference of a circle slightly over three, six, or nine times the length of its radius?
39. Was the Eiffel Tower named for the French Premier at the time of its construction, the engineer who planned it, or the area where it was put up?

40. Was the population of ancient Pompeii noted for its Spartan way of life?
41. What Roman emperor transferred his capital to Byzantium?
42. Where, in Scotland, did the Irish St Columba found a monastery?
43. What's the most important factor in the 'wearing down' of mountains?
44. What would one cook in a sampan?
45. Which metal(s) are vital to survival of the human body — sodium, iron, calcium?
46. Which is the word, specifically, for the yolk of an egg; albumen or albumin?
47. Native soldiers, serving the British in India, were called — what?
48. One St Augustine died in 430 AD; the other, in 604 AD. Which one became the first Archbishop of Canterbury?
49. What flower is a symbol of secrecy?
50. What are the only chessmen that may only be moved in a forward direction?

QUIZ 28
1. What nation developed most of the wrestling holds used today?
2. A cockatrice was a fabled winged reptile, also known as a — what?
3. Why SOLAR plexus?
4. Who, or what, in modern times, first adopted the Red Triangle as his or its symbol?
5. What's notable about the muscle we call 'gluteus maximus'?
6. How many 'i's' in the word for a native of what was once called the Sandwich Islands?
7. Until 1941, Syria was a mandate of what country?
8. What Day is November first?
9. Do devout Hindus eat pork?
10. The word for an emasculated cock bird?
11. What's pidgin English, if not the cooing of doves?
12. Take up to two minutes for this. In how many ways can a family of four be seated at a square table, one to a side?
13. Which country has the southernmost national capital in the world?
14. In which 'Olympic year', between 1899 and 1933 were no such Games held?

15. Scientists are absolutely agreed that which planet has life on it?
16. Myna birds are often a bit pestiferous in the Indo-Pacific region. They are closely related to what other, and familiar, nuisance?
17. Is the spinal cord attached to the brain?
18. It's now Oslo, but previously — what?
19. In English grammar, as what is the word 'an' classified? (Two words.)
20. Another name for fire-dogs, please.
21. What flower is biblically described as exceeding Solomon in glory?
22. What does this suggest — 39.37?
23. Where, notably, have crickets been used as 'watchdogs'?
24. Who tried to transmute base metals into gold, and sought the 'elixir of life'?
25. John Bull is to Britain as who is to France?
26. In five seconds — how many is a dozen baker's dozens?
27. Name a porcine creature.
28. What's the commonest name found in nursery rhymes?
29. Do die-hards live to a ripe old age?
30. What's the original meaning of the word 'asphyxia'?
31. Ozone is a form of what single element?
32. Which is the national language of Peru — Spanish, Portuguese, or an Inca dialect?
33. Is New York the only city in the USA with its own underground railway system?
34. Who was the creator of the character 'Tarzan'?
35. When are lorgnettes used as decoration on certain cuts of lamb?
36. Is a grebe a diving bird, a piece of hoisting apparatus, or an underwater cave?
37. Which is feline — the wolverine, sable, ocelot, hyaena?
38. If a clock strikes both the hours and the half-hours, how many times a day does it strike just once?
39. Which way does the prince move, on a chess-board?
40. Was Caesar Julius' title or 'clan' name?
41. Did the Vikings ever sack Paris?
42. Which struck London first — the Great Plague or the Great Fire?
43. In which book of the Bible is the story of 'The Flood' told?
44. Is the Oxford-Cambridge Boat Race more or less than 100 years old?
45. Where is the Rialto?

46. What move may only be made once (if at all) by a player during a game of chess?
47. What are agarics?
48. Correct this: 'None but the fair deserve the brave.'
49. Did Alexander the Great ever get as far as India?
50. Is a kilogram more or less than two pounds avoirdupois?

QUIZ 29

1. Which major city is on the river Y?
2. On whose feast day did Good King Wenceslas look out?
3. What are gauchos?
4. What kind of person is buried under a cenotaph?
5. What instrument does an orchestra's concertmeister traditionally play?
6. Who uttered the famous words, 'Quick, Watson, I want you!'?
7. Henry Morgan became governor of Jamaica. What was he previously?
8. What was Mussolini's profession before he rose to power?
9. What's a barracuda?
10. What shape are the flowers of ferns?
11. What do geriatricians concern themselves with — the care of the young, the old, or indoor plants?
12. Shostakovitch. A famous composer, sculptor, or chess champion?
13. What do the French lipsmackingly call 'escargots'?
14. What's a cretin?
15. In which game do players 'meld' — canasta, poker, or bridge?
16. What famous aviator's first names were Charles Augustus?
17. Camphor and 'dry ice' both sublimate, doing what?
18. What word for a type of animal comes from the Latin word meaning 'to creep'?
19. With what does 'The Golden Rule' concern itself?
20. What's a pogrom?
21. When the average motor-car is driven backwards, is the mileage so travelled recorded on the odometer?
22. Reverse a word meaning 'spoke abusively' into a word meaning 'bring to addressee or purchaser'.
23. What did rude urchins once yell at bearded men?
24. The first name of 'Treasure Island's' young hero?
25. Is a glockenspiel a festival, a game played with rocks, or a musical instrument?
26. Of what is cannel a variety?

27. Which is on your right, when you face the bow — port, starboard, or stern?

28. Anna Pavlova was one of the greatest female exponents of her art. What art?

29. Where are Nicosia and Famagusta?

30. Why is the mid-day 12 o'clock called 'noon'?

31. A star that flares into far greater brilliance is called — what?

32. The origin of 'salary'?

33. What 'improves each shining hour'?

34. What substance (in its natural state) is sepia?

35. What do nautch girls do?

36. The French words for 'four', 'five', and 'nine'?

37. What's 'bric-a-brac'?

38. Where is Hammerfest?

39. What's the 'opposite of' a prologue?

40. Whose name, notably, is *not* mentioned in the book of Esther?

41. A certain type of writ requires the 'body', or person, to be produced, to investigate the legality of holding him in custody. Its name?

42. Who was on the throne at the time of the Great Fire of London?

43. What's the mayor, or chief magistrate, of a Dutch or Flemish municipality called?

44. Pandit Jawaharlal — Who?

45. What's cacophony?

46. What, notably, does Florence's Uffizi Palace contain?

47. 'The Temple', in London, got its name from what group? (Two words.)

48. The famous physicist, Lord — Who? — was originally William Thomson.

49. Has a natural shade temperature of higher than 140 degrees Fahrenheit ever been reliably recorded?

50. What's different about Greek Kalamata olives?

QUIZ 30

1. What's wrong with a hypochondriac?

2. John Brodribb, a great actor and manager, became Sir Henry — Who?

3. What's the highest mountain in Europe (or mountains, as once a *pair* of volcanoes)?

4. How many more edges than (a) corners, (b) faces, has a cube? (Full answer.)

5. Conversion of one chemical element into another (e.g. copper into gold) is, or would be, called — what?

6. A popular melody is the Barcarole from 'Tales of — Whom?', by Jacques Offenbach.

7. Electricity generated by chemical action (as of acids on metals) is called — what kind of 'ism'?

8. Who painted 'The Light of the World'?

9. To what does the word 'histrionic' refer?

10. When at home, where do Monagasques live?

11. Whom did the Greeks call Hermes?

12. Neat's foot oil. What's a neat?

13. Another name for Sagittarius?

14. Forced 'loans' by his subjects to the King were abolished in 1689. What were these loans called?

15. The capitals of (a) North, (b) South, Vietnam? (Full answer.)

16. Doctors call it 'syncope'. What would most of us laymen call it?

17. 'What', of the Chaldees, was, biblically, the home of Abraham? (Very short word!)

18. Lights, supposedly due to burning marsh gas (methane), seen on bogs, were called — what?

19. Which seashell has been used most frequently in design, paintings, architecture, etc.?

20. Who composed operas about both Macbeth and Othello?

21. What's a unicycle?

22. Tropic of Capricorn. What's meant by 'Capricorn'?

23. Which planet is 'next further out' from the Sun, after Saturn?

24. What was the occupation of a man who wore motley?

25. Two crotchets — or one-sixtieth of a drachm. Each equals one — what?

26. Keats wrote an ode to a Grecian — what?

27. Where is the Franz Josef Glacier? (There's a clue in the name.)

28. The meaning of the phrase 'Par Avion' on an envelope?

29. Into what ocean does the mighty river Lena flow?

30. What does a glazier work with?

31. What's the façade of a building?

32. What does 'ubiquitous' mean?

33. In what are large amounts of fresh water stored, to serve as a supply for a city or other area?

34. Is a native of Nazareth a Nazarian, Nazarite, or Nazarene?

35. The late great Arturo Toscanini was a famous — what?

36. What does 'witch' or 'wych' in the name of a tree tell you about its branches?

37. Who played the title rôle in the classic film, 'The Private Lives of Henry VIII'?

38. Joseph Mallord William — Who? —, the son of a London barber, is considered one of the great English painters.

39. Two enormous lakes in Canada's Northwest Territories: Great — What? and Great — What?

40. What do horologists concern themselves with?

41. What are provolone and mozzarella?

42. Suzanne Lenglen was one of the all-time great champions — in what sport?

43. Of what state is Adelaide the capital?

44. What article, figuratively speaking, does one 'take up', when accepting a direct challenge?

45. If you found wrack on the sea-shore, what would it be?

46. Past one end of the visible light spectrum we get ultra violet rays. How about 'just past the other end'?

47 Two islands, mainly, form what French colony in the West Indies?

48. What kind of cannon (beginning with H) is for firing with high trajectory, and low velocity?

49. Is it true that early 'tennis' balls were black?

50. What film actor changed his name from Archibald Leach?

QUIZ 31

1. A familiar abbreviation for both 'mother' and a beautiful flower?

2. What 'simple' cutting (not excising) operation is serving, increasingly, the purpose of male sterilisation?

3. What are fardels?

4. A man released from prison, who turns out to be a recidivist, does what?

5. What's 'badinage'?

6. 'Hexagon', 'pentagon' — then what?

7. On which coast of Scotland are Montrose and Arbroath?

8. The antonym of 'occidental'?

9. What do we call the station at the end of a railway line?

10. What's a 'homily'?

11. More and more sound recording is now done on audio-tape. Before flat discs were used, *what* was?

12. What country was once swept by a speculative fever popularly called 'Tulipomania'?

13. Covent Garden. The origin of 'Covent'?

14. How do Brazilians spell 'Brazil'?
15. For what grim purpose was phosgene (carbonyl chloride) once used?
16. Another name for the religious order known as the Augustines?
17. The abbreviation for 'Doctor of Laws'?
18. Can you think of a title with four 'a's' in it? (One word.)
19. Does it have to be raining where *you* are, for you to see a natural rainbow?
20. Traditionally, of how many reeds did a pan-pipe consist?
21. Of what is Gruyère a variety?
22. What mountain overlooks Cape Town?
23. Does digested food pass from the stomach into the 'large' or the 'small' intestine?
24. 'Terra' means 'earth'. How about 'cotta', in 'terra cotta'?
25. What gives marble its 'glow'?
26. 'Wine, women, and — what'?
27. What great French liner burned in harbour at New York?
28. Describe the flag of Greece.
29. Where's your instep, on the top of or underneath your foot?
30. What four letters, at the end of the name of a disorder, signify 'inflammation'?
31. On which side of his bride is a groom supposed to stand at a wedding?
32. 'Stone walls do not a prison make, nor — — — —'?
33. The partnership formed between the Nazis and the Fascisti was called the 'Rome-Berlin — what'?
34. Which planet shines with its own light?
35. Benito Juárez is looked up to as a great liberator in what country?
36. Another word for 'congratulations'?
37. Who played the title rôle in the rollicking film, 'Tom Jones'?
38. Which Kipling poem has the shortest title?
39. 'Spelter' is another name for what metal?
40. What were what we now call (postage) stamps once called?
41. Jesus' declarations of blessedness in his Sermon on the Mount are collectively called — what?
42. What delicious fruit, cut open, looks like a melon filled with caviar?
43. Correct this. 'More people enjoy Potknocker's than any other jellies'.

44. In which work were Charles Darnay and Lucie Manette characters?

45. What gas was named after the Sun?

46. In what famous building is Britain's largest bell?

47. 'Hibernation' during summer is called — what?

48. For contributions to what will the names of Doctors Salk and Sabin be best remembered?

49. Physically, what's meant by 'trauma'?

50. It's now Helsinki, but previously — what?

QUIZ 32

1. The male star of 'High Noon'?

2. One inch of rain amounts to about how many tons an acre — 1, 10, 100, or 1000?

3. The name of what mythical river gave us a word meaning deadly? Or, if you prefer, what word?

4. In fiction, the name of what plant was used by an apparent fop who was actually a daring adventurer?

5. What's the word for the verb, or verbal part, of a sentence?

6. The author of 'The Wealth of Nations'?

7. Spell the word meaning 'agreement among a number of people', and beginning with 'con'.

8. Which was not a Shakespearian play — 'Richard I', 'Richard II', or 'Richard III'?

9. Basically, what are listed in a pharmacopoeia?

10. Which is further north — Detroit, Michigan, or Windsor, Ontario?

11. Who referred to sleep as 'a gentle thing, beloved from pole to pole'?

12. Are the leaves of the beetroot plant good to eat?

13. To a South African, what does 'IDB' most probably suggest?

14. Is St Peter's, in Rome, a church or a cathedral?

15. Who was the father of Henry VIII?

16. We know the river Tevere better as the — What?

17. What mistake is most frequently made, in cooking most vegetables?

18. What's the connection between Yale locks and Yale University?

19. What do we call a brief published biography of a person just deceased?

20. What's meant by 'circa 1656'?

21. To the nearest whole year, how long does it take money to double, at 5 per cent annual compound interest?

22. Which is strictly correct — Welsh rabbit or rarebit?
23. Correctly pronounce 'impious'.
24. What flower got its name from flesh?
25. What have these names in common — Sabinian, Sisinnius, Formosus, Lando, Zachary, and Constantine?
26. What garden was the scene of the betrayal of Jesus?
27. What, with an area of over 41,000 square miles, and a population of about 11 million, long abbreviated its name as, simply, O?
28. Does the term 'deal' apply to 'soft' woods (like pine and fir) or hardwoods like birch and oak?
29. Is the 'g' in 'lugubrious' pronounced like 'g' in 'got', or 'j' in 'jot'?
30. What's the word for 'rebound' when applied to a bullet (or other projectile)?
31. Which has the greater population — Austria or Australia?
32. If a Frenchman says 'Bienvenu', what would an Englishman say, in his place?
33. What Asian country's name means 'Land of the Pure'?
34. What mineral was the original source of radium?
35. What, nothing to do with bees, are hives?
36. What do tympanists do?
37. One of the mightiest species of trees was named after Sir James Douglas, first governor of British Columbia. What kind of tree?
38. What, originally, were sequins?
39. What's the largest shadow any man has seen?
40. The author of 'The Old Man and the Sea', and the name of the late great actor who starred in the film made of it? (Full answer.)
41. What country calls itself 'Norge'?
42. On what part of his person would a man wear a cummerbund?
43. A girl named Gladys Smith left Toronto for early Hollywood and became what long-famous movie star?
44. 'Silver bells, and — what?'
45. Where are the Ploesti oilfields?
46. What would you most probably have in mind to see, were you to visit Agra?
47. Can the 'Northern Lights' be seen on a clear night?
48. What juicy fruit's name means 'seedy apple'?
49. In films, Ingmar and Ingrid — who?
50. What place is associated with Bernadette?

QUIZ 33

1. The surname of the Napoleonic marshal who founded Sweden's present royal house?
2. The name of Lake Ontario starts and ends with identical letters. To which other of the Great Lakes does this apply?
3. What are the two colour varieties of the liqueur called Chartreuse?
4. What now, fortunately, less active, terrorist organisation is referred to as the 'KKK'?
5. In the game of draughts (checkers) what must you do if your opponent insists upon it?
6. What, respectively, is left when you take the butter from cream, the cream from milk, and the curds from what's left?
7. Are there now more or less Maoris than when Europeans first met them?
8. Where is the famous Sunset Boulevard?
9. Is a chasuble a religious vestment, a poor investment, or an investiture?
10. A four-letter word, meaning 'burden, responsibility'?
11. What great river carved out the mile-deep Grand Canyon?
12. If a man wears huaraches at all, he'll almost certainly wear two. What are they?
13. The word for putting something solid together, layer upon layer (e.g. plywood)?
14. Where is Lake Eyre?
15. Lord — who? — was Prime Minister when the United States declared their independence of Great Britain?
16. What's the process of heating milk to about 140 degrees F., to inhibit bacterial growth, called?
17. The emerald is green. How about the topaz?
18. The plurals, respectively, of 'noose', 'moose', and 'goose'? (Full answer.)
19. To what and whom does 'the ploughman leave the world'?
20. Name a gastric enzyme with a six-letter word. (Middle two, 'PS')
21. A French politician's name is applied to profile portraits in solid black and white. What name?
22. Apart from paying for them, what must one do at the time of purchasing travellers' cheques?
23. Name two parts of the body with single words ending with 'x'. (Full answer.)
24. Which popular nursery rhyme mentions three different animals?

25. What and where is Adrianople, and after whom was it named? (Full answer.)
26. On what island is 'downtown' New York City?
27. Washing out river-gravel and sand, in search of alluvial gold, is popularly called — what?
28. What was the symbol adopted by the Free French in World War II?
29. Into what, assuming correct diet, does the body convert starch?
30. What handsome city could be called 'the capital of Mormonism'?
31. What have chalk, marble, and limestone in common?
32. Can pure yellow phosphorus be safely exposed to the air?
33. What were 'Stukas'?
34. What great film made 'Harry Lime' a famous name?
35. A postage stamp that has not been postally used, or marked, is referred to as — what?
36. Correct this. 'This data is unacceptable.'
37. In what vocation was Jesus trained?
38. Name the over-600-mile-wide bay on the south coast of Australia?
39. German attacks, on what country in each case, brought Britain into what became World Wars I and II? (Full answer.)
40. Are all pure metals, apart from gold, 'silvery' or 'grey' in colour?
41. The term used for enforced racial segregation in South Africa?
42. 'Procrastination' comes from the Latin word 'cras', meaning — what?
43. Normally, what passes through the 'bronchial tubes'?
44. 'A — what? —, a — what? —, my kingdom for a — what?'
45. Who, on the 'silver screen', enhanced her reputation in the rôle of 'Diamond Lil'?
46. A 'sacrificial' chess-opening move is referred-to as a — what?
47. Correct this. 'No-one may leave their seat!'
48. Who was the first man to orbit the Earth, in 'space'?
49. What causes those brown stains on cigarette-smokers' fingers?
50. Of two types of bacteria, bacillus and coccus, which is 'rod-shaped'?

QUIZ 34

1. The plural of 'manservant'?
2. Doing what, with spilled salt, is supposed to 'prevent bad luck'?
3. Who, originally, were the inhabitants of 'pandemonium'?
4. What's the taal, or language, called that's spoken by the 'Dutch' in South Africa?
5. Large quantities of millet are grown in India. For what purpose?
6. The Gulf of Bothnia separates what two countries?
7. Identify all four of the sports in which these terms, respectively, are used — 'Fore!', 'LBW', 'Service!', 'On guard!'
8. What's Gouda noted for?
9. With the aid of what instrument is the light, from heavenly bodies, for example, 'broken up' and examined?
10. 'A rag, a — what? —, and a hank of hair'?
11. What happens to 'light rays' when refraction occurs?
12. 'Forewarned is — what?'
13. What's Carrara noted for?
14. To what northerly seaport in Russia did convoys bring enormous quantities of needed supplies, during World War II?
15. What's the traditional outdoor gathering-place (e.g. on New Year's Eve) in New York City?
16. The common name for a fly in the larval stage?
17. Where is plutonium mined?
18. What kind of people are fortunate enough to use both hands with equal skill?
19. What does '-ectomy', at the end of a word, signify?
20. Lamas; llamas. Tibetan monks; S. American beasts of burden. Which are which?
21. An antonym for the adjective, 'obscure'?
22. Is insulin produced by the pancreas or the thyroid?
23. Which is called the 'Red Planet'?
24. What word means both a whip and a certain short hair?
25. Where does 'a tide in the affairs of men' lead?
26. After whom, for two obvious reasons, was a type of air-force safety-vest nicknamed?
27. What's a fane?
28. Of what is the nutty-flavoured 'Amontillado' a principal dry variety?
29. A very rare species of what is called the 'Glory of the Sea'?
30. In certain warm countries, where the pace of life is a bit slower, the word 'mañana' is popular. What does it mean?

31. Would one ride in, eat, or cook in, a brioche?
32. The word for a written statement confirmed by oath?
33. What famous American cape is named for a fish?
34. Name four seas named for colours. (Full answer.)
35. The larch (or tamarack) is a coniferous tree, but an unusual one for what reason?
36. What word, ending with '-late', means 'surrender'?
37. Mail, or post, sent overseas, but not by air, is referred to as — what?
38. Buying, building, and/or operating — what? — made Mr Conrad H— famous?
39. The Sudbury area in 'Northern' Ontario is noted for producing a large share of the world's — what metal?
40. What debt was acknowledged by the bells of St Martin's?
41. 'Mater' and 'Pater', we know about. Distinguish between 'maté' and 'pâté'.
42. Which gospel-writer is reputed to have been a physician?
43. Name all three of these trees. They respectively sound like a product of combustion, a strand, and a pelt.
44. Who played the title rôle in the film, 'Becket'?
45. What's wrong with this sentence? 'You may invite whoever will come'.
46. What gas, when inhaled, temporarily gives one a strangely metallic-sounding or high-pitched voice?
47. What's the Ob?
48. (Three seconds.) On which side of the wearer is the bow worn on a man's hat?
49. What's unusual about the Watussi tribesmen?
50. On whose side was Japan in World War I?

QUIZ 35
1. What do Italians mean by wishing you 'Buon Natale'?
2. Which is colder — zero Centigrade or Fahrenheit?
3. Which planet has the 'Giant Red Spot'?
4. A diver coming up too suddenly, dangerously causing nitrogen bubbles to collect in his system, suffers from — what?
5. What 'braes are bonnie'?
6. Through what instruments can one see varied patterns formed from odd bits of coloured materials?
7. Which well-known type of liqueur has a strong chocolate flavour?
8. Which important Canadian city was first named Bytown (after a Colonel By)?

9. The song says, 'You gotta have — what'?
10. Which plant has been placed in the wrong 'family' — cauliflower, radish, lettuce, cabbage, mustard, turnip, Brussels sprouts?
11. Who was 'in the arms of Morpheus' under a haystack?
12. What major American city is frequently referred to as Gotham?
13. Where, in the Crimea, was a fateful 'Summit Meeting' held during World War II?
14. Where is the famous Copacabana Beach?
15. What's the plural of 'axis'?
16. The winged staff of Mercury, used in some areas as a symbol of the medical profession, is called a — what?
17. What did Russions traditionally use when making tea?
18. What did Sir Francis Galton do that led to problems for criminals?
19. When Columbus sailed, who was king of (a) Spain, (b) England?
20. Name three present-day national capitals, beginning with C (as we spell them.)
21. What normally keeps the bones of the spinal column from 'rubbing against each other', or impinging on nerves that branch out between them?
22. In later years, what was added to a Roman numeral to signify multiplication by 1000?
23. Who immediately preceded Nikita Khruschev in power?
24. Could brandy finally be made, starting with apple-juice?
25. What's meant by 'inert' in reference to a gas?
26. Where is the rand the monetary unit?
27. What's the generic name for bindweed?
28. Of what is Fredericton the capital?
29. What's unusual about this sentence? 'Oh gee, Kay, I see a queue!'
30. What nomenclature is applied to hurricanes and typhoons?
31. With what symbolic gesture did Pontius Pilate waive responsibility for Christ's death sentence?
32. Do oysters lay eggs?
33. What fruit, its name beginning with Q, is often made into jelly?
34. Seville and Valencia are particularly identified with what fruit?
35. Correctly pronouce 'heinous'.
36. Two things brought fame (and money) to the urban centres of Nevada. One, uniquely, was legal gambling. The other?

37. In what ocean are the Andaman Islands?

38. Which two states in the USA were named for Queen Elizabeth I? (Full answer.)

39. What Hollywood star started life as Bernard Schwartz?

40. What's 'brimstone'?

41. Sir Winston's father and son shared what first name?

42. Forgetting about size, which U.S. city could loosely be called that country's Montréal?

43. Which card game has a doubly alcoholic name?

44. One sees 'EIIR' frequently. What does the 'R' stand for?

45. Who wrote 'The Origin of Species'?

46. What flower with the same name as a colour may have a different colour?

47. In one word, what was the specific fruit with which Eve tempted Adam?

48. Correct this. 'To completely enjoy soccer one should know all the rules'.

49. Where is Lerwick? (Country name insufficient.)

50. What popular fruit is closely related to the plantain?

QUIZ 36

1. Who or what 'sat in the Cardinal's chair'?

2. What are argon, krypton, neon, and xenon?

3. What's the calm centre of a hurricane called?

4. Where, in Germany, was an important 'Summit Meeting' held, at the close of World War II?

5. An edge (e.g. of a plank) cut at a slanting angle, is called — what?

6. What does one mean by 'to cry wolf'?

7. To whom largely is the credit given for discovering the antibiotic qualities of certain moulds?

8. What's a 'sorbet'?

9. What kind of song is called a berceuse?

10. Two customs, distinctively Spanish, rhyme. One may occur periodically, the other daily. What are they?

11. What's an altercation?

12. The upper edge of a boat's side once supported cannon. Hence, it's called — what?

13. Sir Joseph Wilson Swan's invention was made practical by Edison. What was it?

14. Not everyone likes medlars. What are they?

15. Another word for 'lasso'?

16. In what years did the USA enter the two World Wars? (Full answer.)
17. Within two, how many letters in the Hawaiian alphabet?
18. What edible Oriental bean, of many uses, is now being ever more widely cultivated?
19. What late famous 'Press Lord' and politician was born in Canada, and named Max?
20. Who 'discovered' Cuba?
21. Elizabeth, the Queen Mother, was known as — what? — prior to her marriage to the then Duke of York?
22. A community — where? — has experienced colder temperatures than any other.
23. 'Fifteen, two; fifteen, four; and a pair, is six'. In what game is this often heard?
24. What tall building was tragically struck by an aeroplane some years ago?
25. Correct this. 'She spoke to Jim and I'.
26. What bird's mouth can 'hold more than its belly can'?
27. What's the most famous building on the most famous Pennsylvania Avenue?
28. Where are Shanklin and Ventnor?
29. Which of the disciples of Jesus was re-named 'Rock'?
30. What important area in Australia was named for an important area of Britain? (Not a city.)
31. When Ike was seen with Winnie, who were they likely to be?
32. Beer is made from malted barley. What beverage is widely made from tomatoes?
33. Who was Captain Ahab's mortal enemy?
34. What noted author became Sir Pelham—?
35. A combination of oil and water (usually aided by a third substance) is called — what?
36. 'Thrice' is 3 times. What's a 'trice'?
37. Of what country is Lower (or Baja) California a part?
38. What are stamp hinges?
39. Who were the 'three men in a tub'?
40. The estate of the Duke of Beaufort gave its name to what popular sport?
41. A bishop's head-dress and a carpentry joint share what name?
42. Of what was Dr Nkrumah very much the 'boss'?
43. One — what? — 'doesn't make a summer'?
44. What four-legged creatures respectively bray, whinny, 'laugh', and low? (Full answer.)

45. The word for a geographical index or dictionary?

46. What's a carboy?

47. Tristan and — ?

48. What condiment does the name Dijon bring to mind?

49. 'Will you love me in December, as you did in — '?

50. Correct this. 'They hung him at daybreak'.

QUIZ 37

1. What then new tactic temporarily won the island of Crete for the Nazis?

2. Which common word is derived from the name of the supreme god of the Norsemen?

3. What word, rhyming with 'shoot', means 'debatable'?

4. What's supposed to be at the 'end of the rainbow'?

5. Brigadiers-general, brigadier-generals, or brigadiers-generals?

6. With what is forensic medicine concerned?

7. To what larger sea does the Sea of Azov connect?

8. What is friable soil?

9. What do 'bonsai' enthusiasts do? Notably in what country? (Full answer.)

10. What is the preferred pronunciation of 'wassail'?

11. What are Protozoa?

12. Which country had Prime Ministers named Venizelos and Metaxas?

13. Fundamentalists believe in the literal accuracy of what?

14. Compounds of which of these gases play a major part in the manufacture of conventional explosives — helium, chlorine, nitrogen?

15. The word that's the name of what country applies to certain timbers, the ridges of corduroy, and marks raised on flesh (as by a whip?)

16. Four adjectives, please — all beginning with 'j' — and implying good humour or gladness.

17. What sets off so-called 'tidal waves'?

18. How many times during a day do a clock's hands simultaneously point straight up and down?

19. Distinguish between 'diagnosis' and 'prognosis'.

20. What term is applied to various rocks of volcanic or similar 'molten' origin?

21. A better-known name for the substance, phenol?

22. What do imbibers do?

23. Of what country is the 'Brabançonne' a national song?

24. Which is India's longest river?

25. Whom, on the screen, did Warner Oland, and then Sydney Toler, repeatedly portray?

26. What gelatinous substance is made (notably) from sturgeons' bladders?

27. What's the antonym of 'wax'? (Tricky!)

28. Where is one most likely to find Seminoles — in Florida, in the kitchen, or bubbling out of the ground?

29. Where is the Gulf of Taranto?

30. Of what is a firkin a measure?

31. In connection with traditional performances of — what? — is Oberammergau famous.

32. What islands are separated from a mainland by the Pentland Firth?

33. Who ordered the Sun to stand still — Moses, Joshua, or Abraham?

34. What's the 'ring of light' called that's seen at a total eclipse?

35. A world-famous Spanish concert pianist. Jose — ?

36. Does 'Burley' apply to pipe-tobacco, pottery, or a type of sail?

37. Painting on a plaster surface (usually before it's dry), with powdered pigments mixed in water, is called — what?

38. How many ounces in a Troy pound?

39. Mussolini borrowed from the early Romans his symbol of an axe surrounded by a bundle of rods, called — what?

40. What is a menhir?

41. Rearrange the letters in the name of the present capital of Japan to form that of the former one.

42. The term for a postage stamp without little holes punched along its sides?

43. What is a foible?

44. The plural of the word for 'a single male animal reproductive cell'?

45. We use the seeds, oil, and fibre of what non-tropical cultivated plant (not a member of the 'grass family'?)

46. Titus Oates created a hubbub in 1678 with a story of a religious plot involving the assassination of — whom?

47. What Fisher substituted a Taylor for a Reynolds?

48. Which is heavier — a quart of fresh water or a quart of sea water?

49. What long world-famous 'crooner' was actually named Harry Lillis — ?

50. The peninsula occupied by Spain, Portugal, and Gibraltar?

1. A mango, when ripe, is a delicious fruit. What's a mangosteen?
2. Which Canadian prairie province actually has a sea-coast?
3. The word for artificially supplying water to crops on otherwise arid land?
4. What's the German word for 'Germany'?
5. What, besides a geometrical figure, is called 'rhomboid'?
6. What is oscillation? (Not the electro-magnetic kind!)
7. A felloe, a fellow, and a fellah. A wheel-rim, a comrade, an Egyptian peasant. Which is which?
8. What do we mean by 'quondam' — questionable, former, or an earthwork to hold back water?
9. 'Gone With the Wind', the famous novel. How many pages in the regular edition — 714, 1024, 1,764?
10. What's the word for a judicial inquiry into cause of death?
11. Is strabismus an eye condition?
12. What kind of sea creature is a medusa?
13. Mountains in Crete and near the site of ancient Troy share what name with a girl 'sweet as apple cider'?
14. William Paterson (expectably a Scot!) founded what famous institution?
15. Do any snakes bear live young?
16. The name of Jacob's youngest son is applied in a general way to the youngest son of any family. What's the word?
17. Name Agatha Christie's most famous detective.
18. There are many alloys, but what's the special word for any alloy of mercury?
19. What does Aylesbury, in England, have in common with Long Island in New York State?
20. What's a Borzoi?
21. What notorious (very!) dry area in the USA shares both nomenclatural and situational characteristics with the Dead Sea?
22. What solvent makes a solution a tincture?
23. If cattle are bovine, what are sheep?
24. A collective name for these three daughters of Zeus — Clotho, Lachesis, and Atropos.
25. Another name for muriatic acid (HC1)?
26. Dobbin for a horse: what for a fox?
27. What did the Tommies make out of 'Ca ne fait rien' and 'Il n'y a plus'? (Full answer.)
28. What is opulence?
29. What was known as the Wehrmacht?

30. What common flower got its name (beginning with 'A') from something in the heavens?
31. What's liverwort?
32. Which of the Disney 'Snow White' dwarfs was beardless?
33. Within ten, about how many pieces are put together to make a violin?
34. Define 'vaunted'.
35. What do we call a legislative body consisting of a single house instead of the usual two?
36. In which ocean could one find sea-shells near the Seychelles?
37. What kind of metrical foot consists of an unaccented syllable followed by an accented one (like the word 'defy')?
38. If Mrs Rees has six daughters, and each has one brother, how many children does she have?
39. What is meerschaum, used in making pipe bowls; and what does the name literally mean? (Full answer.)
40. In one word, what — in speech or writing — is called 'hyperbole'?
41. How do Americans pronounce 'Derby', as in 'Kentucky Derby'?
42. A capital city in two words, using only five different letters?
43. What's the effect of adding the prefix 'A-' to a word?
44. How many sons were born to George V?
45. Strictly speaking, is an invidious remark an unjust or envy-provoking one, a confidential one, or a vague one?
46. What did an autogyro most nearly resemble?
47. The flowering plant 'Love-lies-bleeding' is an amaranth. What's meant by 'amaranthine'?
48. In what resort area is Antibes?
49. To what are the biblical names Jeroboam, Rehoboam, Nebuchadnezzar, etc., applied?
50. The name of the goddess of retribution has become part of the language. Name?

QUIZ 39

1. How many of Henry VIII's legitimate children succeeded him to the throne?
2. On what would you be disconcerted not to find a ripcord?
3. What do we call the projecting edges that keep a train's wheels on the rails?
4. Cremona, Italy, is particularly famous for what product?
5. Marcus — Who? —, a Roman Emperor, is remembered

for, among other things, his philosophic work, 'The Meditations'?

6. The late Edward G. Robinson, famous for his screen portrayal, among others, of gangsters, was not born in America — but where?

7. What highly unusual award was won by the heroic Captain Upham of New Zealand?

8. What small country owns the world's largest island that isn't classed as a continent?

9. Where would Tamil be most useful as a language — Northern Sri Lanka, New Guinea, or New Zealand?

10. 'Verb. sap.' How do we usually say it in English?

11. Which is thrown furthest, at the Olympic Games — the javelin, the shot, the hammer, or the screwdriver?

12. Sir Arthur — who? — wrote the play, 'The Second Mrs Tanqueray'?

13. What did curiosity kill?

14. Amundsen, Ellsworth, and Nobile crossed the North Pole in an airship. Its name?

15. What ancient North African country had a great ocean liner named after it?

16. To what do the terms 'triassic' and 'jurassic' refer?

17. A Duke of Clarence was drowned in a butt of — what?

18. Is 'switching' from exalted speech to trivial called athos, bathos, or pathos?

19. In what Himalayan country is Katmandu?

20. What food is served at a 'Barmecide feast'?

21. The quagga is now probably extinct. What creature did it most resemble?

22. Everyone knows that a knell is the sound of a bell — but particularly — when?

23. What common name means 'pearl'?

24. What are Lions, Kiwanians, Rotarians, and Kinsmen?

25. What 14th century conqueror claimed descent from Genghiz Khan?

26. Which of our letters, as it appears in the Greek alphabet, resembles *our* letter 'P'?

27. Which king of Northumbria was made a saint?

28. What's meant by taking 'umbrage'?

29. To a cook, what's a roux?

30. What's cordite?

31. 'The widow's mite'. What was it?

32. What one word means a tailless animal, part of a horse's 'foot', a kind of button, and part of a railway installation?

33. On a three-masted vessel, which is the mizen (or mizzen) mast?
34. Does a yataghan belong in a collection of robes, headgear, boats, or weapons?
35. Arthritis attacks the joints. What are Arthropods?
36. With what kind of wooden peg or pin are two pieces of wood often joined together?
37. Who was the founder of 'antiseptic' surgery?
38. The word for the right of succession's belonging to a first-born (usually, son)?
39. Brecon, in Wales, was the birthplace of what great actress of the past?
40. Literally, what are tenterhooks used for?
41. What does *desiccated* coconut mean, literally?
42. What is batik?
43. Who said to his Love, 'Then live with me and be my Love.'?
44. Are kiwis native to both Australia and New Zealand?
45. If Charybdis was the whirlpool, what was the rock?
46. 'A to Z' could apply to the two apostles called James, parentally. Why?
47. What's a swagman, to a native of, say, Brisbane?
48. Name, in two words, the moist lining of various body cavities, like the mouth.
49. Could one get drunk, partaking of arrack?
50. 'A Roland for an —'?

QUIZ 40
1. What gave malaria its name?
2. The popular word for an African big game hunting expedition?
3. What fabled bird rose from its own ashes?
4. Who, in history, is the best-remembered person of the Barca family?
5. What regulates the action of a mainspring in a watch? (Begins with 'e'.)
6. Of what talented, but barbaric, people was Quetzalcoatl one of the chief gods?
7. What Hindu word, meaning 'curtain' or 'veil', was applied to the seclusion of women in India?
8. What was built during the first century AD, to accommodate over 80,000 spectators?
9. In music, what's the fourth part of a quaver called?
10. Whose death did Shelley lament in 'Adonaïs'?

11. Incense is burned in a thurible, otherwise known as a — what?
12. Of what is Kabul the capital city?
13. Chaps aren't always males, or sores on a lip. What else?
14. Who purport to 'read' the bumps on their gullible clients' heads?
15. What's the word for a reference collection of synonyms, phrases, or quotations, etc? (Not 'dictionary'.)
16. The same word is applied to a young member of a noble family and a shoot used in grafting. What word?
17. What's notably 'different' about Charles Dickens' 'Mystery of Edwin Drood'?
18. Strictly speaking how long does an ephemeral insect live, or disease last?
19. Is something amorphous small, smelly, or shapeless?
20. In a circle, what's a vector?
21. What Italian town's associated with both cheese and violets?
22. Of what was Vulcan the Roman god?
23. To what would one normally apply a pomade?
24. What are Caslon, Bodoni, Kabel, Garamond, and Cheltenham?
25. By means of what special slender entwining shoots do many climbing plants cling to surfaces?
26. In what vehicles, according to what we most frequently hear, were aristocrats taken to the guillotine?
27. What word, meaning 'alien' is applied to a species of falcon?
28. Which was the first British possession to issue postage stamps?
29. Where's your uvula?
30. The late Jacob — who? —, a clever but controversial sculptor, was of Polish origin, was born in the USA, and lived in London.
31. Another name for the aubergine?
32. In which country is Lagos?
33. Another name for saltpetre (or potassium nitrate)?
34. What's the occasion called when the Sun is furthest from the equator?
35. What gourd has proved useful to the making of certain smoking-pipes?
36. What's the word for the viscous essential substance of which the cells of living organisms principally consist?
37. Portree is the most important centre on which of the larger of the British Isles?

38. A drug that's been used on fingernails to prevent children's biting them. Bitter — what?
39. What type of jam got its name from the Portuguese word for a quince?
40. When the Israelites left Egypt, they wandered through Sin. The — what? — of Sin.
41. Name the great, but chivalrous, Mohammedan enemy of the Crusaders.
42. What highly inflammable substance, then used in making film, caused many early cinema fires?
43. To which nation do we owe the invention of safety matches?
44. The great painter, Diego Rodriguez de Sylva y —, died in 1660. Name?
45. A great Russian oil centre on the Caspian Sea. Name?
46. In which of the gospels do we find the story of the five loaves and two fishes?
47. Colloquially, how do we refer to what a doctor calls an axilla?
48. Who was probably the most famous Scots entertainer of the first half of this century?
49. Where do some believe unbaptised infants, and people who lived before Christ, go to when they die?
50. What, belonging to Naboth, did Ahab covet?

ANSWERS

QUIZ 1

1. Hats. 2. Bronze. 3. Tetanus. 4. Huguenots in France.
5. Spatula. (Dull-bladed implement.) 6. Belgium, Netherlands
Luxembourg. 7. A wax separated from certain whale-oils.
8. Foot-racing. 9. Ho Chi Minh. 10. Denmark's mainland.
11. I. 12. Bavaria. 13. Conga. 14. (Grasshopper-like, noisy)
insect. 15. Cambodia. 16. No (e.g. 40-foot basking shark!)
17. Mary III. 18. Hansen's disease. 19. China. 20. Samuel
Taylor Coleridge, and S. C-T. 21. William II of England.
22. Vitamin C. 23. No. (Mussels, giant clams, etc.)
24. 'Mother of pearl'. 25. Normal cavities in (usually, bony)
tissue. 26. Canada. (Uncountable!) 27. Dormer. 28. France!
(Corsica.) 29. Fist. (Pugnus.) 30. Corded fabric or ribbon.
31. Means both 'join together' and 'split apart'! 32. Epic.
33. Geese. 34. No. 35. Northernmost point on British
'mainland'. 36. Caliban. 37. Poisonous snake: soft leather
shoe. 38. Leon Trotsky. 39. The moose. 40. Honey. (Re-
gurgitated by bees.) 41. Plant. 42. The man. (But not if he'd
been forty.) 43. Cockatoo. 44. One's self. (Rolls under another
bed. Truckle-bed.) 45. Romans. ('Popes' incorrect.) 46.
Leisure, weight, heinous, reign, species, etc. 47. Crocodile or
alligator. 48. Canada. 49. 38. 50. Michelangelo.

QUIZ 2

1. Horses front, cows hind, legs first. 2. Soviet. 3. Pitt, the
Elder. (Earl of Chatham.) 4. Plain. 5. Norway. (Mid-1800's).
6. Yes. (Some, many times that length.) 7. The Hindenburg.
8. Spartacus. 9. For this purpose; or, in this case only.
10. It wasn't. (Set adrift in Hudson's Bay.) 11. Yes: try it.
12. W. Somerset Maugham. 13. Originally, the Spanish
dollar was a 'piece of eight', worth eight reals: the rest is
arithmetic. 14. Tom, the piper's son. 15. The first is a
Christian fletcher. 'Nuff sed?' 16. St Peter. 17. Yes (but not
too long: married at 18.) 18. Nitrogen and hydrogen. 19. Yes
(inexplicably, so far.) 20. Gastric ulcer. 21. Yes (e.g. various
sharks.) 22. Tine. 23. (Dried) bud. 24. Charles II (Catherine.)
25. Yes. (Shakespeare said to have visited, with actor troupe.)
26. Sir H. Rider Haggard. 27. Filigree. 28. Duenna. 29.
Writes material for publication under another's name.
30. Self. 31. Kingfisher. 32. (Kibo peak of) Kilimanjaro
(19,340 ft.) 33. Titian. 34. (Like salmon) leave sea to spawn

in fresh water. **35.** Sleep. **36.** Aye-aye. **37.** Outriggers. **38.** 'Fluid' includes 'gaseous'. **39.** The roc. **40.** Rolling, or shifting, logs. **41.** None. (Fastest, slightly over 22.) **42.** Nuts! **43.** (Idolatrous) worship of Virgin Mary. **44.** Aquarium. (Tiny fish.) **45.** Citrus. (Citrous.) **46.** (Peter Paul) Rubens. **47.** Yes, literature (in 1953.) **48.** (North Island) New Zealand: hot springs, geysers, etc. **49.** Sweden. **50.** Arizona.

QUIZ 3

1. Yes. (about 100 miles N. of Nairobi.) **2.** Farming. **3.** 105. **4.** Rangoon (by over 300 miles.) **5.** That they could pass through it unharmed. **6.** None. (Different John.) **7.** Aleutian Is. **8.** Ends: 'Hamlet'. **9.** Cosmonauts. **10.** The Balearic Is. **11.** Twice. **12.** Rembrandt (van Rijn.) **13.** K2 (Godwin Austen.) (Kanchenjunga a close third.) **14.** No. (Chemist: druggist.) **15.** Yes. **16.** Fanatic. **17.** Coati-mundi. **18.** Medicine. **19.** Leonardo da Vinci. **20.** Cabbage. (Caboche.) **21.** Gambling (card) game. **22.** The. (old symbol for 'th' somewhat resembled a 'y'.) **23.** Christian. **24.** Moses'. **25.** Franklin D. Roosevelt. **26.** Leprosy. **27.** Queen Anne. **28.** Fulcrum. **29.** Crimean. **30.** The right side. **31.** Assassinated (bunglingly.) **32.** Powdered iron (or filings.) **33.** No: a fowl rumour! **34.** Hamelin. **35.** Anemometer. **36.** A gratuity (often serving as bribe.) **37.** Straw, warts. **38.** Nota bene. **39.** Rockies. (Named for rock formation.) **40.** Without having left a will. **41.** Brother. **42.** Nostalgia. **43.** Insects. **44.** Basil Rathbone. **45.** W. **46.** Panama. (Made in Ecuador.) **47.** Fools' gold. **48.** Ravens. **49.** Brazil. **50.** Several.

QUIZ 4

1. Swimming. **2.** Minestrone. **3.** (About) 73 per cent. **4.** An arrow. (Friar Schwarz.) **5.** Mandarin (or Japanese) oranges. **6.** The Sun. **7.** Unlikely; but mongoose would die. **8.** Leather. **9.** From 'raisin', French for 'grape'. **10.** No. (Fungi, for example, don't.) **11.** Noah and family. **12.** A liqueur (flavoured with anise.) **13.** Tax collecting. **14.** The Mackenzie (incl. Peace River, 2,635 miles.) **15.** Lusitania. **16.** Sluggards. **17.** The Salic Law. **18.** Faithful. **19.** Buddhists. **20.** Bitter, pungent. **21.** 1917. **22.** Bechuanaland. **23.** 'Burma Road'. **24.** Yes. **25.** (Capital) Malagasy Republic (Madagascar.) **26.** Stonehenge, by far. **27.** Pandanus. (Screw-pine.) **28.** Ashore (bury in sand.) No. **29.** Grape skins. **30.** George III. **31.** Carbon. **32.** 3. **33.** Blond. **34.** Endocrine. **35.** No. (Jogs to avoid islands.) **36.** Benjamin Disraeli. **37.** (a) none, (b) none. **38.** They 'split' the pot. **39.** Males. **40.** Snakes. **41.** Spawn. (Mycelium.) **42.** Over 500. **43.** Fish: (flat-bottomed) boat. **44.** 'Vittles'. **45.** Islam. **46.** Mental disorders. **47.** Territory surrounded by that under a different political administration. **48.** St Lawrence. **49.** Points. **50.** George Arliss.

QUIZ 5

1. Blenheim Palace. **2.** Having extra fingers or toes. **3.** None. **4.** Ten. **5.** Red, white, and blue. **6.** Neither, really; but do let light through. **7.** James I. (VI, of Scotland.) **8.** Struck blind. **9.** Alaska and Florida. **10.** Carp. **11.** Yes. (Robert Anthony.) **12.** Pups. **13.** Mumps. **14.** The Boy Scouts. **15.** Condominium. **16.** More. (Atmospheric pressure greater.) **17.** Wet. **18.** Alliteration. **19.** Mauna Kea (peak of island of Hawaii, itself an enormous volcanic mountain.) **20.** Crocodile tears. **21.** Helium. (Hydrogen lightest element.) **22.** Shepherd. **23.** Physics, Chemistry, Medicine (physiology), Literature, Peace. Economics added in 1969. **24.** One. **25.** (Only) C.D. **26.** Tonga. **27.** Wear it. (Near Eastern robe.) **28.** Tungsten (symbol W.) **29.** Alexander Korda, Merle Oberon. **30.** (Admiral) Jellicoe. **31.** Metonymy. **32.** Son, off whose head William shot the apple. **33.** Denmark. **34.** Farouk. **35.** Standing. **36.** Mignonette. **37.** Liechtenstein. **38.** Ginger. **39.** 3 a.m. (Think about it.) **40.** Mosques. **41.** Yes. (A stretch upstream, between Montréal and Lake Ontario.) **42.** Fur seals. **43.** Obsequiousness. **44.** Russian rivers. **45.** No. **46.** Peach. (Nectarine, too.) **47.** Seven. **48.** Dr. Watson. **49.** (Goldilocks') three bears. **50.** Tang: gnat.

QUIZ 6

1. February. **2.** Sir Joshua Reynolds. **3.** (Aegean) island group. **4.** 5. (Fishes, amphibians, reptiles, birds, mammals.) **5.** Skater. (Probably not 100 metres, though.) **6.** 30. **7.** San Salvador. **8.** Charles Kingsley. **9.** Valhalla. **10.** In his own country. **11.** Franz Lehar. **12.** Rungs of ship's 'rope ladder'. **13.** One of three astronauts killed in tragic space-capsule fire during a test on the ground. **14.** Only when you have no other container in which to offer it! **15.** Amaryllis. **16.** They're kneecaps. **17.** Alexandria. **18.** Birds yes, fishes no. **19.** God willing. (Deo gratia.) **20.** Ibis (bird: Egypt. Ibex are wild goats.) **21.** Hemp from untwisted old rope. **22.** Genoa. **23.** 36 (of 88). **24.** Henry VIII. **25.** Trash. **26.** No. (Kosciusko, 7,328 ft.) **27.** They have antlers, too. **28.** U.S.S.R. **29.** Calling it 'goverment'! **30.** Asteroids. ('Rocks' of various sizes, in zone between orbits of Mars and Jupiter.) **31.** The sitting part. **32.** Mrs Dwight D. Eisenhower. **33.** March. (Mars.) **34.** Yes (if diet deficient in lime.) **35.** (Bone) in forearm. **36.** Dormouse. **37.** (Lago) Titicaca. (12,506 ft. above sea level.) **38.** Gorilla. **39.** (Province and city of) Spain. **40.** Waltz. **41.** About 1,500 tons. **42.** (Silent) film star: Italian. **43.** (Central north coast of) Australia. **44.** Old Stone Age. **45.** Albert. **46.** Cashew! **47.** Y. **48.** Bering. **49.** 1963. **50.** 'Ribbled'.

QUIZ 7

1. Sequoia. **2.** Yes. (1877). **3.** Eyelid. (They move sideways.) **4.** Dehydration. **5.** None. (They're virulent satires.) **6.** Plays set of bells (now generally, by keyboard.) **7.** Bisque. **8.** (John and John Quincy) Adams. **9.** The foiling of Guy Fawkes' 'Gunpowder Plot'. **10.** Guide-books. **11.** Turkey (from America.) **12.** Biennial. **13.** Fruit-kernels. **14.** Tree. **15.** Assassinated. **16.** Dante. **17.** Colorado. **18.** Projection on horse-shoe to prevent slipping. **19.** Quite a few (sleepwalkers.) **20.** (First Earl of Oxford and) Asquith. **21.** Shrewd ones. **22.** Yes. **23.** Georges Clemenceau. **24.** Outward. **25.** Resin. **26.** Green. **27.** 'Creation'. **28.** George Frederick Handel. **29.** (North African) mongoose. **30.** Organic (chemistry.) **31.** Yes. **32.** Tongues. **33.** Latex. **34.** Yes. **35.** B.C., and P.E.I. **36.** David Copperfield. **37.** Rebus is pictorial. **38.** Good Friday! **39.** Neil Armstrong. **40.** Far from it. **41.** Switzerland. **42.** Spent. (Spanish gold coin, two pistoles.) **43.** Bouillabaisse. **44.** Artificial rubber (developed in Germany during World War II.) **45.** Fish. **46.** Opaque water-colour painting. **47.** Walloons. **48.** Cedar. **49.** Fruit, 'beans' (of carob tree.) **50.** Millicent.

QUIZ 8

1. An asp. **2.** The mother lode. **3.** Italian child; also figure of the infant Jesus. **4.** Never. **5.** General pardon. **6.** Pegasus. **7.** Itinerary. **8.** Vellum, calfskin: parchment, sheepskin. **9.** Jul-Aug: Dec-Jan. (No other.) **10.** Catherine the Great, of Russia. **11.** Mulberry leaves. **12.** Baikal, U.S.S.R. (6,365 ft., in one place.) **13.** (Variety of) shark. **14.** Not dachshund pup! Doberman pinscher. **15.** Arletta, a tanner's daughter (illegitimately.) **16.** Rossetti. **17.** Any (two-dimensional) shape. **18.** Abdicated (1399.) **19.** Symptom. **20.** No. **21.** Swarm of bees. **22.** 30. **23.** (Tsarist) Russia. **24.** Measles, mumps. (The others, bacteria.) **25.** 1588. **26.** Yes. **27.** Dominicans. **28.** Copy or 'steal' the literary or artistic work of others and pass it off as their own. **29.** The 'infernal regions'. **30.** Oman. **31.** The White Rabbit. **32.** The Hope (Diamond.) **33.** Fireworks. **34.** Apparent. **35.** City of London. **36.** Regiment. **37.** Bort, coarse diamonds. Borscht, beetroot (etc.) soup. **38.** (Accra.) Ghana. **39.** Love (zero) (from 'l'oeuf'.) (Duck, in cricket, similar.) **40.** Featherweight. **41.** Rime. **42.** Horseshoe-pitching. **43.** Newfoundland. (Site of large airport.) **44.** Pterodactyl. ('Winged fingers'.) **45.** Blind or shutter. **46.** Cowpox. (Vaccinia.) **47.** Nervous system. **48.** In scallop shell. **49.** Start with 'C'. (Cotswolds, Cheviots, Chilterns.) **50.** Anthrax.

QUIZ 9
1. To anyone, plucking instead of bowing violin string. **2.** Jupiter. **3.** 28. **4.** Australia-New Zealand Army Corps. **5.** Doge. **6.** Cathedrals. **7.** Pretty well. Ssssh! **8.** Persian. (Pae jamah, leg covering.) ('Hindi' acceptable.) **9.** Polymers. **10.** Enjoying an issue of spirits. **11.** Jack-rabbits. **12.** Saudi Arabia. **13.** Well over 1,000! **14.** MIX (1009.) **15.** The cup or platter used by Christ at the Last Supper. **16.** Paintings, line engravings. **17.** Hydrophobia. **18.** Take your choice: paper's scarce. **19.** Yes. **20.** The English Channel (to a Frenchman.) **21.** Wine (and revelry.) **22.** Cabochon. **23.** (Giant) tortoises. **24.** (Overlooking) Rio de Janeiro. **25.** Apple pulp (e.g. for cider.) **26.** Calendar-adjustment. (11 days 'lost'.) **27.** 'Kubla Khan'. **28.** Music. **29.** Yes. (Lamarck, for one.) **30.** They're 'twin 'cities, contiguous. **31.** Sorry, no such year. 1 AD followed 1 BC. **32.** Above (but pods bury themselves.) **33.** Remained neutral. **34.** Bolivia, Paraguay. **35.** Tobacco. **36.** Torpedo-boats. **37.** Mistress. **38.** Shoe-makers. **39.** The Sun. (Umbra, shade.) **49.** Drink. (A green tea.) **41.** Air. **42.** (Plant) drug. ('Deadly nightshade'.) **43.** Labyrinth. **44.** Songs. (Best known, 'Aloha Oe'.) **45.** Baseball. **46.** (Wild) honey. **47.** Reverence. **48.** Australia. **49.** Scrubbing decks. **50.** Eat and enjoy it. (Mould of meat or fish, baked in a crust.)

QUIZ 10
1. 130. **2.** Shakespeare's. **3.** Latin 'quaetio'; reduced first to 'qo' then to 'Q' with a little circle under it, then (carelessly, perhaps) to the present '?'. (Exclamation mark, similarly, came from the joyful interjection 'Io!') **4.** 'the Lord be thankit'. **5.** Public vote on a given matter. **6.** Queen Victoria. (Regina.) **7.** Scarab. **8.** Grizzly bear. **9.** 56. **10.** From.

11. Slaughterhouse. 12. Shade. 13. Yes. (Germany.) 14. Almost an island. 15. Eruption of Vesuvius. 16. Pluto. 17. Fish believed extinct for millions of years. 18. Trite, hackneyed, commonplace, etc. 19. China. 20. Caulking. 21. The lac insect. (On certain tropical trees.) 22. None. (Amphibian, not mammal.) 23. Illumination. 24. John Cabot. 25. (The earliest, Christian) English poet. 26. Kensington Gardens. (Peter Pan.) 27. Small earthenware pot. 28. Robert Burns' sentence 'The best laid plans . . .' 29. Humming-birds, by far. 30. They lie. 31. Never. Leis. (Poi is taro starch, used as food.) 32. None of them (31-28.) 33. Motorcycle accident. 34. A soft cheese. 35. Minnie. 36. Book. 37. Elizabeth I. 38. Dandelion (dents de lion, in reference to leaf shape.) 39. One, always. 40. Graphite (carbon.) 41. 12. (All true adult insects have 6 each.) 42. The rudder, below water, steers the boat. The tiller is a lever wherewith to operate the rudder. 43. Muscular. 44. Juno. 45. Bedlington! (Northumberland.) 46. Pacific (when any of it gets that far!) 47. The boxer, Joe Louis (Barrow.) 48. Lebanon. 49. Certain seaweeds. 50. The 'dark' part of such a moon would block the view of any star.

QUIZ 11

1. Human. 2. Substance used to kill plants (e.g. weeds, unwanted grass.) 3. Anthony Hope. 4. Cornucopia. 5. (New, volcanically formed) island (off Iceland.) 6. Meat roasted in small pieces. 7. Borneo. 8. In them it doesn't remain constant. 9. Capricorn. 10. Anatomy, structure. Physiology, function. 11. George V. 12. Leached from land and washed away by rivers. 13. Haemoglobin. 14. Certainly. (As much as 24 hours a day in *our* winter.) 15. One tenth. 16. Lots! 17. All treebark products. 18. Instruments of torture. (St Catherine.) 19. (James) Ramsay Macdonald. 20. Machinery, for fear of job loss. 21. Egg (ovum.) 22. (Ware of) copper, coated, (by fusion,) with silver. 23. Percy Bysshe Shelley. 24. For uniform understanding everywhere. 25. Kidneys. 26. Malay. 27. Mark Anthony. 28. Pinnace, pinnacle. 29. (Admiral Richard E.) Byrd. 30. Principles of heredity. Genetics. 31. Hummingbirds. 32. In Spain. 33. A yoke. 34. Moraines. 35. A 'bird in the hand'. 36. Yes, and more! 37. Ravenna. 38. Conquest by the Normans. 39. My order is correct. 40. Nowhere. 41. Egotist. (Egoist is selfish.) 42. Quite a few more. 43. Charles II's. 44. Males. Females receive and regurgitate it into offspring's mouths. 45. (Had) dug a (narrow) Suez Canal. 46. (Picardy

is in northern) France. **47.** Phlegm. **48.** Seventy degrees. (Total, a right angle.) **49.** Plants (both food, and decorative.) **50.** A week. (7 night.)

QUIZ 12

1. A lawbreaker. **2.** L.A., by far. **3.** David. **4.** Never. (Greeks didn't use them in their calendar.) **5.** Light meal, often of cold meats. **6.** Mildly. **7.** A type of wide knot in a man's necktie. **8.** No. **9.** The reigning sovereign. **10.** Well over 30. **11.** No. (Elliptical orbit.) **12.** 72. **13.** Central America. (Unflavoured.) **14.** 'Eyes'. **15.** Conic sections. **16.** Type of 'sea-cow'. **17.** White. **18.** To the death! **19.** Once 2 feet or more across. **20.** Carbon, oxygen, hydrogen. **21.** Brothers and/or sisters. **22.** Bacilli. **23.** Aachen. **24.** France. **25.** (Emma, daughter of Richard, Duke of) Normandy. **26.** White rice. **27.** Backwater. **28.** Fancied resemblance to pine-cones. **29.** Samoyed(e). **30.** Hood and trunk. **31.** Monks. **32.** No. The guilder. **33.** Puccini. **34.** Slender animal, related to the lemur. **35.** Sorry. Gutenberg was not English. Nor, of course, were Chinese who did it considerably earlier. **36.** Brown. **37.** Distilling wine. **38.** Gourds used (shaken) to provide rhythmic sound in Latin-American music. **39.** Christopher Columbus· (Cristobal, Colòn.) **40.** Jericho. **41.** Yes. At high elevations, of course. **42.** Musculus: little mouse! **43.** Yes! **44.** Fungi. **45.** 7th (AD 664.) **46.** Beans. **47.** Invisible! (Bats are mammals.) **48.** Corfu. **49.** Stanley Baldwin. **50.** In the sea. (Fish.)

QUIZ 13

1. 73,000. **2.** 'In the human breast'. (Pope.) **3.** Popeye the Sailor. (Olive Oyl.) **4.** Roads were long neglected, and even torn up. **5.** Eating. **6.** John Harvard. (Founded university.) **7.** Ditto. (Back of arm.) **8.** Semi-precious stone. (A tinted quartz.) **9.** Trek. **10.** Lichen. (Fungus and alga together.) **11.** Sand. **12.** Provide much shade. **13.** Whole milk. **14.** Cumin (cummin.) **15.** Flatulence. **16.** Many do. (Using the legs as toothpicks??) **17.** River (now Menderes, in Turkey.) **18.** Begging. **19.** Tepees, wigwams, wickiups. **20.** No. **21.** Population. (Human.) **22.** Honshu. **23.** Ivan (IV) 'the Terrible'. **24.** Island off Chinese coast. **25.** USA. **26.** Potatoes. **27.** (Rectilinear) quadrilateral. **28.** Yes. (Often great distances.) **29.** Uranus. **30.** Cobalt. **31.** Women, Cambridge. **32.** States. **33.** Alaska. (Mt. McKinley, 20,320 ft.) **34.** Count of Monte Cristo. **35.** When 6 hours slow (fast.) **36.** Florence.

(Florin, now 10p.) **37.** China. **38.** Hong Kong. **39.** Wilhelmina. **40.** Small bunch of (fragrant) flowers. **41.** Travel. **42.** Water (power.) **43.** Rank. **44.** Trumpeter. (His 'lip'.) **45.** Large hanging fan. **46.** Haemophilia. **47.** Hardwicke. **48.** Sudan: larger. **49.** Deliquescence. **50.** Scorpion, mite. (Arachnids.)

QUIZ 14

1. Elm. **2.** Algeria, Tunisia, Libya, Egypt. **3.** Shortest distance between two points. **4.** Poliomyelitis. ('Infantile paralysis'.) **5.** San Marino. (23.5 sq. miles.) **6.** 'False step': social error. **7.** Yes. (Marciano 'timed' at over 120.) **8.** George Bernard Shaw. **9.** Enormous banquets. **10.** Yes. (Some, occasionally, four miles.) **11.** Edward VII, (Sixpenny dull violet, overprinted I.R. OFFICIAL.) **12.** Tyre, Sidon, etc. They were originally Phoenicians. **13.** 'Vitamin B'. **14.** Rudyard Kipling. (Recessional.) **15.** Drawn by 3 horses abreast. **16.** The tilt of the Earth's axis. **17.** Asia. **18.** 24 furlongs is 3 miles. **19.** Diaeresis. Pronounce the vowels separately (Ah-ee-dah.) **20.** Hackles. **21.** Ararat (16,946 ft.) **22.** Aluminium. **23.** No. (Separate Canadian territory.) **24.** Sorry. The 'Father of His Country' was childless. **25.** Lapland is a region, not a country. **26.** 'Arabic' numerals. **27.** Tibia. **28.** Three score years and ten. **29.** Fez. **30.** Bikini. **31.** N. and S. Carolina. **32.** Which was to be shown, or proved. (Quod erat demonstrandum.) **33.** A half. **34.** Hippopotamus. **35.** Gold. **36.** (Short, like) sparrows' (for seed-eating.) **37.** Transposing. **38.** Boris Karloff. **39.** Jews. **40.** (Variety of) apple. **41.** Fauna. **42.** Small fleet. **43.** Nobody. (Caesar wrote 'three parts'.) **44.** 90 degrees North. **45.** Two. (Opposites total 7.) **46.** Genocide. **47.** Canada. **48.** Marlene. **49.** Ireland. **50.** The Bahamas.

QUIZ 15

1. (Early type of flintlock) gun. **2.** Hawaii. **3.** Hot winds. (About two months, in spring.) **4.** Pulsating bleeding. **5.** Equivocation. **6.** Newf'ndLAND. (NOT NewFOUND-land.) **7.** Ductility. (Not malleability, which it also possesses.) **8.** Yes, literature. **9.** Molten iron. **10.** Mass. **11.** A zoo. (Not native.) **12.** Latin. **13.** Guatemala. **14.** Mexico. **15.** Graphite. **16.** Casein. **17.** Insulin, and its control of diabetes. **18.** They don't. (No atmosphere to create friction.) **19.** Neither can fly. **20.** Her right. ('Outside', yes — but not acceptable!) **21.** A pint. **22.** Petroleum. **23.** Nova Scotia. **24.** An extremely 'hot' bottled sauce. **25.** (In) Belgium. **26.** (Huge game) fish:

waterproofed canvas. **27.** Charlemagne. **28.** (Rosette or other) hat ornament. (Worn as badge, or part of livery.) **29.** 170 — 65 below zero to 105 above. (Neither, actually, a record.) **30.** Beige. **31.** About 350 million! **32.** Sinecure, soft job: pedicure, 'manicure' for feet. **33.** Maltese crosses. **34.** Found. **35.** Ran (most of the way) from Paris to India. **36.** On head. **37.** Spanish moss. **38.** (Two-edged) Scottish sword. **39.** O-H. **40.** Orca; or 'killer' whale. **41.** Cousins. **42.** The Bull. **43.** Nowhere. (3rd person used.) **44.** Victoria. **45.** White. **46.** Talkative. **47.** Thick downy feathers under wings. **48.** Multilingual. **49.** 11¼ seconds. (Nine 1¼-sec. intervals.) **50.** A minor sin or misdemeanour.

QUIZ 16

1. Snakes. (Could have hundreds.) **2.** (Thomas Robert) Malthus. **3.** Papyrus. **4.** (a) kor, (b) corps. **5.** 'Nevermore!' **6.** Garibaldi. **7.** Jerusalem. **8.** (A delectable chicken and potato) soup (served cold.) **9.** Poland. **10.** Eggs. **11.** 'O'. **12.** The banns. **13.** Berlin! **14.** American Indians. (U.S. Southwest and Mexico.) **15.** Rochester, Minn. (Mayo Clinic.) **16.** Linden. **17.** 90 per cent! **18.** C, (Ascorbic acid.) **19.** Aardvark. (Aardwolf second.) **20.** Ramie (fibre) and hominy (treated Indian corn.) (Both answers needed.) **21.** Benny Goodman. **22.** Burning is oxidisation. Rust is iron oxide. It is already 'burned'. **23.** A plant. Leaves and shoots of Egyptian privet (Lawsonia inermis.) **24.** 21. **25.** On Japanese ships (or material dealing with them.) **26.** Yes. (Its square equals sum of squares on the other two sides.) **27.** Emperor of Ethiopia. **28.** None. (Angora goats.) **29.** Yes. (I've personally seen a 1,100 lb. specimen hauled out of the Fraser River, and a 700 lb. one from the Columbia!) **30.** Sweet nothing. **31.** Yellow. **32.** India (now, of course, partitioned.) **33.** (Depends where it is!) In itself, no. (A scar.) **34.** Chili (pepper.) **35.** (a) Sage, (b) savory. **36.** Before. **37.** Ersatz. **38.** Stem! **39.** Singhalese. **40.** Stitch in the side. **41.** Zither. **42.** Iceland. **43.** Chignon. **44.** Grit they've swallowed. **45.** Quite a few. **46.** (Made with oxidised) linseed oil. **47.** (Metal) tray. **48.** Domrémy. **49.** The 'Bounty' mutiny. **50.** Yes. (But hardly a simple matter!)

QUIZ 17

1. Papoose. **2.** Pastoral, rustic. **3.** Gladstone. **4.** Norway. **5.** Towards where it's high tide. **6.** Membranes enveloping lungs. **7.** Louis XVI. **8.** Castile soap. **9.** No. (Mangroves are.)

10. Both fish. 11. Greasy little musical instruments. 12. That of the Earth's circumference. 13. Edward, Duke of Kent (fourth son of George III.) 14. (Crystalline) mineral. 15. Tasmania. 16. They 'spit' drops of water at them, with amazing accuracy. 17. British soldiers. 18. A type of cheese. 19. Octopus, squid, cuttlefish. 20. 16. 21. No. He did visit there, and wrote about it. 22. Upper shell of tortoise, crustacean, etc. 23. Singular. (Everyone IS . . .) 24. Yes (but not necessarily vice versa.) 25. Certain pores in plants. 26. Highly unlikely, with that many offspring. 27. Ellice. (Pacific island group.) 28. Dancing. (Fred Astaire.) 29. (For a few) gold in the Yukon. (The Klondyke.) 30. Seven. (A-G.) 31. 1911. 32. High. 33. Black. (Ebony.) 34. Anise. 35. About 140,000. 36. (Sir John Everett) Millais. 37. Jesus. 38. (German town of) Landau. 39. The leek and the daffodil. The 'dragon'. 40. Went down (6¾ miles) to ocean bottom (1960.) 41. Charles II. 42. Munchausen. 43. Omnivorous. 44. 17. 45. One under 'legal age', a minor. (If right, congratulations! Common error.) 46. Doppler. 47. God be wi' ye. 48. Second. (Josephine, a widow.) 49. Barnacles. (To certain whales, too.) 50. Olive branch.

QUIZ 18

1. Almonds. 2. B. 3. Jack Johnson. 4. Two Roosevelts, Coolidge, Hoover. 5. Taxidermist. 6. Rain-water. (No other potable water there.) 7. Daphne du Maurier. 8. Hurling a spear. (An ancient device.) 9. Montréal. 10. The author has been told it's delicious. 11. Sleep. (French railway sleeping-car.) 12. That so-called experts can be fooled. (It was a hoax.) 13. Socrates'. 14. Hot. (July-August, when Sirius, the 'Dog Star', rises with the Sun.) 15. Cortège. 16. Lord Darnley. (Mother, Mary Queen of Scots.) 17. 12 lbs. 18. Portugal. 19. Gypsies. 20. They possess both male and female reproductive organs. 21. Extra-sensory perception. 22. Specialise in skin disorders. 23. Acid. 24. The white (nearly twice as much.) 25. Cow. (Latin, vacca: French, vache.) 26. None. (Beograd.) 27. On an island. (Sjaelland.) 28. Suez (about 87 miles to Panama's slightly over 50.) 29. Fifteen p.s.i. 30. The Black Hand. 31. Alcatraz. 32. Gary Player. 33. 'Pie de grue', a *crane's* foot, was a mark used to denote succession. 34. (The one) 'from Armentières'. Parley-voo? 35. Far less. 36. Italy. 37. No. (Oesophagus) (Others; tomb, 'windpipe'.) 38. Cutting corn or grain (to fall evenly.) 39. Lapis lazuli. 40. Experimental aeroplane, intended to fly by flapping its wings.

41. Incorrectly. 42. Lady. 43. Two-man spacecraft. ('Twins'.) 44. Taxüng. 45. None. (Invisible.) 46. Not vice versa. 47. Mississippi. 48. ('Signal Hill' near) St John's, Newfoundland. 49. Incubation. 50. Perkin Warbeck.

QUIZ 19

1. Rhodesia. 2. 9 hours. 3. Not vice versa. 4. Amino-acids. 5. 'Taste-buds'. 6. Carbon monoxide. 7. Sauce. 8. All fours. 9. Third. (Tissue damage.) 10. It's cut down: new 'trees' shoot up. 11. Swastika. (Hooked cross.) 12. Diana. 13. One's vegetable garden. 14. Albania. 15. One. 16. Two. 17. Jons Jakob Berzelius (Swedish chemist.) 18. His father and uncle. 19. They ARE fish. 20. The Arabs (about 900 AD.) 21. Ponce de Leon. 22. Synonym. 23. Never. Before Confederation, the term applied to Ontario (up the St Lawrence.) 24. Using everyday language. 25. HMS Beagle. 26. I. 27. Easter and Christmas Islands. 28. Knits (stink.) 29. Cutting blubber from whales. 30. Wattle. (National flower.) 31. (Transparent, crystalline) rock. 32. Newfoundland. 33. The Mahdi. 34. You shouldn't. You're breathing it. 35. Wars of the Roses. 36. Boris Spassky. 37. Eva Braun. (Just before their deaths.) 38. Blazing, flaming. 39. Cain. 40. Alberta. 41. Barcarole. 42. Acetic. 43. In the heat of the Sun. 44. Solomon. 45. Chess. (Forces a draw.) 46. Homer. 47. The siege there. 48. No. 49. The 'mouth' end, only! 50. (Prince Otto von) Bismarck.

QUIZ 20

1. Coconut. (Coco de mer.) 2. Jesus wept. 3. Dr Mossadeq. 4. Punic Wars. 5. Encircling wall; or open space within it. 6. Barbados. 7. 'I go on forever'. (Tennyson, 'The Brook'.) 8. Ferrule. 9. (a) Nightingale, (b) Wren, (c) Drake, Hawke, or Byrd! 10. £30. (Spent £20 and £4.) 11. Scotland. 12. Joseph Priestley. 13. On the 'big island' (Hawaii) in the Hawaiian Is. 14. Thames! 15. USSR. 16. Yes. (E.g., in the soil, and in digestive tract.) 17. Years. 18. Place, near Milan. 19. Oignon. 20. The Maelstrom. 21. Iraq. (Near Hilla.) 22. No. (In fact, there are 4 or 5 different species in the Pacific.) 23. A wasp. 24. The Jolly Roger. 25. Brass. 26. Bee: (wasp acceptable.) 27. Ride. (Carriage.) 28. Three eighths. 29. Meat 'tenderiser' (unseasoned!) made from papaya juice. 30. Silicon. 31. Ver-BATE-im. 32. Bacteria and viruses. 33. Q. 34. H, N, S, X, Z. 35. Asbestos (fire *proof!*) 36. Sad. 37. Yorkshire. 38. Keratin. 39. Leonardo da Vinci. 40. Wheat. (Original types.) 41. Catalyst. 42. a-RYE. 43. American Declaration of Independence.

44. Part, or all, of a circle. 45. Baton. 46. Yes. 47. Curved legs on furniture. (Notably Chippendale.) 48. Eleven. 49. Men. 50. Victoria.

QUIZ 21

1. Ambergris. 2. Prometheus. 3. Spurs. (Spiked discs.) 4. Atlas. 5. Shibboleth. 6. Drunkenness. 7. Iceland: (considerably.) 8. Sir Thomas Malory. 9. A cheese is no statesman. 10. Seaweed. A jelly (used in medicine, foods, etc.) 11. Yes. (Occupied about 140 BC.) 12. Angola (due east.) 13. Think about that date! 14. The veldt. 15. Boadicea. 16. They grow on vines. 17. Basket (usually paired) carried by donkeys, etc. 18. Napoleon (1797.) 19. Made 'boats' with them. 20. No. He was taken there from Britain by marauders. 21. Four. 22. It became a republic. 23. Spaghetti. 24. Uterine. 25. Usury. 26. Wampum. 27. Having two wings. 28. Yes. (Delicious, and expensive! Hand-gathered.) 29. Iris. 30. Its cry. 31. Painted (it.) 32. (Battle of) Blenheim. 33. Julius Caesar. 34. (True) artichokes. 35. Nicaragua. 36. Touch. 37. Press-ganging (British), or shanghaiing (U.S.) 38. Energy-providing 'fuel'. 39. Yes! (Ice crystals, sometimes.) 40. Iron. 41. Volatile. 42. If that marsh-bird has its way, its own insides. 43. Italian hors d'aeuvres, or appetisers. 44. (State of) Virginia. 45. Anything written in cipher. (Cryptograms.) 46. (Despite common mispronunciation), two. 47. (Certain) fish. (E.g. Siberian blackfish.) 48. Tail. 49. (Large, noisy) beetle. 50. Yes.

QUIZ 22

1. Basketball! 2. Alfred the Great. 3. Yes. (Even twice that.) 4. Thinner. 5. By males, in a 'pouch'. 6. Sponge-cake surrounding whipped cream. 7. Languages (devised for international use.) 8. (Fish-eating) duck. 9. Fossils of sea-creatures. 10. Affirm. 11. Maoris. 12. Iron. 13. ('Scrambled') and by radio. 14. Juggernaut. (Jagannath.) 15. Named after people. 16. The Senate. (Very little 'power', compared with Roman or U.S. Senate.) 17. Lepidoptera. 18. Mid-Atlantic: (over 10,000 miles.) 19. Yes. (Quite a few metals do.) 20. Neither, (The female bites.) 21. Repent at leisure. 22. Props. (Properties.) 23. 'Peter Pan'. 24. Gubernatorial. 25. Pantograph. 26. Noodles. 27. Furs. 28. Dental 'enamel'. 29. Slave. 30. Sir Alec Douglas-Home. 31. Beetles. 32. Bituminous. 33. The moon. (Originally, more light for pilgrims to travel by.) 34. USA. 35. That of the Holy Trinity. 36. Madame

Butterfly. **37.** To a doctor (heart specialist.) **38.** Loops, spool. **39.** Topaz. **40.** Québec (50 per cent larger.) **41.** Nothing! (Scores can be kept on paper.) **42.** Henry IV, V, and VI. (Four did it, later.) **43.** The books he wrote. **44.** Calender. (Colander is a kitchen strainer.) **45.** Not yet. (U.S. runs it.) **46.** Yes. (So is 'monosyllabic'.) **47.** Tête-à-tête. **48.** (Perfect) diamond. **49.** Pharaoh. **50.** Henry I.

QUIZ 23

1. Migraine. (Hemi-cranium.) **2.** Smoke it. (Peace-pipe.) **3.** Tower. **4.** (Acetyl-salicylic acid.) 'Aspirin'. **5.** 1,285-1,295. **6.** (Scarf worn over) heads. **7.** 10,000. **8.** Eaten (delicious!) **9.** Famous 'Siamese twins'. **10.** (White) marble. **11.** Sidereal (year.) **12.** Polders. **13.** Yes. **14.** Marathon. **15.** To keep his guardsmen from wiping noses on them! **16.** Plenty of company. **17.** Trowel. **18.** Really? **19.** Raccoons. **20.** 'Lincoln green'. **21.** Lovely as a tree. **22.** Spendthrift; wasteful. **23.** A 'great fish'. (No mention of whales!) **24.** An inch. **25.** Gross. **26.** Greece. **27.** 2100! **28.** It means 'uncuttable' (indivisible.) We now know better, don't we? **29.** 'Good wine needs no bush'. **30.** First man given transplanted heart. **31.** Wheat. **32.** More. (Approx. every 76 years.) **33.** Mortal. **34.** Venice. (Native huts on stilts in swampy areas.) **35.** Legumes. **36.** Ham **37.** Six. (September, May.) **38.** 'Cold-blooded'. (Reptiles.) **39.** Calcium. **40.** Mountainous areas of B.C. and the state of Washington. **41.** Worship Allah. (Mohammedans.) **42.** Logs. **43.** Castor oil. **44.** None. **45.** U.K. **46.** Her great tennis ability. **47.** (Plum-like, astringent) fruit. **48.** Muscatels. **49.** No. (Troyes, France.) **50.** Cathay.

QUIZ 24

1. They use kayaks. ('Kulak' is a term for a Russian peasant-farmer or trader in produce.) **2.** Hydrogen. (Matter's simplest form.) **3.** Colombia. **4.** Andrew Carnegie. **5.** Literature. **6.** Caledonian. **7.** Musk-deer. **8.** One behind another. **9.** They bear live young. **10.** Cleanliness. **11.** X-rays. **12.** (Stigmas of) crocus (sativus.) **13.** Two: Portuguese. **14.** 10. **15.** Survival of the fittest. **16.** None. **17.** Nautilus. **18.** Brother and sister. **19.** Cleopatra. **20.** Holland, France. **21.** Paddle-like. **22.** (Type of) wild pig. **23.** 'Oh'. (Try listing them!) **24.** Condition of perplexity. **25.** Parrot. **26.** Miracle! **27.** (Greek.) Means 'under' (dermis, the skin.) **28.** 2. (Father and son.) **29.** (Bishop's) chair or throne. **30.** Canada's highest. (19,850 ft.)

31. Lack of protein in the diet. 32. At the back (where the optic nerve 'ends'.) 33. Never. (Although he believed he'd reached the Orient.) 34. Lac Léman. 35. Followed armies, selling provisions to the soldiers. 36. Kent. 37. The Sherpa who climbed Mount Everest with (Sir) Edmund Hillary. 38. Formosa. 39. Smallpox. 40. Lettuce; women. 41. Slice specimens extremely thinly, for examination. 42. Penny-farthing bicycle. 43. Dance (Brazilian origin.) 44. Harlem Globetrotters: itinerant team of talented basketball players. 45. Nullarbor. 46. A small country in the Balkans: part of Yugoslavia since 1919. 47. Tap water, by far. 48. Italy. 49. Manna. 50. (Niccolo di Bernardo dei) Machiavelli.

QUIZ 25

1. Many have. 2. Michelangelo's. 3. Artists. 4. Waterspout. 5. Munster. 6. Slightly over 8 ft. 11 ins. (Bob Wadlow, of Illinois.) 7. Science of teaching. 8. Hawks. 9. (Spiral cavity of inner) ear. 10. Basalt. 11. Kelp. 12. Edward VII. 13. Mexico City (over thrice as great.) 14. Quakers. 15. Yes. (Violently, 1707.) 16. Over a door or window. 17. Blood's circulation. 18. 'Prepare to shed them now'. 19. Japan (or Japanese restaurant.) 20. A die. 21. All three. 22. No. (Orville, 1948.) 23. Gas-detection in mines. 24. 36. 25. Bbls. 26. Hernia. 27. Beri-beri. 28. Vertebrae. 29. Canaveral. (For a while, called Cape Kennedy.) 30. Some of today's vessels are too large to pass through it. 31. Top to bottom. 32. Law. 33. Hamilton. 34. Tip of tail. 35. Rebelling against machinery by throwing wooden shoes into it. (France.) 36. Banyan. 37. Ceres. (I gave you a hint!) 38. It isn't. It's mined. 39. Yes, a little: mainly minerals. 40. 15,781; right on. 41. Stratford! 42. Thailand (Siam.) 43. More (often considerably so.) 44. Mansard, double-sloped roof: Hansard, record of Parliamentary proceedings. 45. A puck. 46. (Pith of a) palm tree. 47. (Tomas de) Torquemada. 48. Surgeon. (Operation on skull.) 49. Bicuspid. 50. Simultaneous discharge of guns.

QUIZ 26

1. Six. 2. Cotton-seed oil. 3. Edward, the 'Black Prince': Cornwall. 4. Depends, doesn't it? 5. Game: (fore-runner of lawn tennis.) 6. 'Stirrup' bone (stapes) in ear. 7. (Blue) dye. Also its plant source. 8. Roman coins. 9. Heifer. 10. Operetta. 11. KNOWLEDGE of matters 'supernatural'. 12. Currency that may legally be offered as payment. 13. New Guinea: (over 1,600 miles.) 14. By volcanic heat and pressure.

15. Rafael Sabatini. 16. World War I. 17. Alarm bell or signal. 18. Not on your Nellie! 19. Voltaire. 20. Mohammedan calendar. 21. Dipsomaniac. 22. 20. (5, 7, 8.) 23. Archaeologist. (Others: extinct life forms, and public records, respectively.) 24. None. (Earth, air, mixtures. Water, compound. Fire, incandescently oxidizing gas.) 25. That of lemons. 26. Morphine. (Morpheus.) 27. David Niven. 28. Drunk. (Sometimes very.) (Strong spirits.) 29. Quorum. 30. Bloodstream. (White corpuscles.) 31. Kentucky. 32. Napoleon. 33. Enigmas. 34. Straight hair. (Consider a watch-spring!) 35. Nowhere. (In danger of extinction!) 36. (West coast of) Greenland. 37. Oporto. 38. Olympus (9,550 ft.) 39. Eggwhites. ('Eggs' not good enough.) 40. Arbour. 41. Apples. 42. James I (VI of Scotland.) 43. Holly. 44. Mountainous. 45. A (highly intelligent) breed of dog. 46. Water. (Vacuum, not at all.) 47. Longfellow. 48. Hemlock. 49. A magnum. 50. Carbon dioxide.

QUIZ 27

1. Magnesium. (E.g. flashbulbs.) 2. Martinet. 3. Forest. 4. 1,000. 5. Originally used to cut points on quills, for writing. 6. Clifton (Suspension.) 7. (a) putting things off (b) lying. 8. Whom. 9. Toronto. (Indian.) 10. 'Parmesan'. 11. Afghanistan. 12. January 1, 1901. 13. The Sun. 14. Brazil. 15. I serve. 16. One. (Angles always total 180 degrees.) 17. Trees. 18. 'Red Indian', narghile (pipe), seat on elephant, Indianan, respectively. 19. Deficiency of iodine in one's diet. 20. William Shakespeare. 21. More. 22. Hasn't yet. (Stevenson!) 23. Officer in charge of his superior's horses. 24. Dispossesses. (Others?) 25. Aphrodisiac. ('Love'-potion material.) 26. Doldrums. 27. Women. 28. Goat(ee). 29. Curry powder. 30. Stone of Scone. 31. Certainly. Maple sugar is! 32. Of unsound mind. 33. About 1 in 100! 34. He wasn't. (He was incarcerated.) 35. It isn't. (Obtained from oceanic flora and fauna.) 36. It appears to 'play dead', although some say it simply faints! 37. Extremely rare ones! (They're shell-like clappers used by Latin dancers.) 38. Six (forty-four sevenths approx.) 39. The engineer. (Gustave Eiffel.) 40. Hardly! 41. Constantine the Great. 42. Iona. 43. Ice. (Expansion during freezing.) 44. Just about anything, if one elects to cook in a smallish Oriental boat. 45. All of them (and others!) 46. Neither. (Egg-*white* is the albumen.) 47. Sepoys. 48. The second one. 49. Rose. (Sub rosa.) 50. Pawns.

QUIZ 28

1. (Ancient) Egypt. 2. Basilisk. 3. Radiating nerve-fibres. 4. YMCA. 5. Body's largest. (In buttocks.) 6. Two. (Hawaiian.) 7. France. 8. All Saints' Day. 9. Yes (but not beef.) 10. Capon. 11. ('Business English') a jargon used in the Far East. 12. 24. 13. New Zealand. 14. 1916. 15. Earth. 16. Starlings. 17. Yes. 18. Kristiania. 19. Indefinite article. 20. Andirons. 21. The lily. 22. Inches in a metre. 23. China. 24. The alchemists. 25. Marianne. 26. 156. (12 x 13.) 27. Pig. 28. Jack. 29. Not necessarily: just stubborn in opinion. 30. Stoppage of the pulse! 31. Oxygen: (in three-atom molecules, instead of the usual two.) 32. Spanish. 33. Definitely not. 34. Edgar Rice Burroughs. 35. Never. ('Specs on a handle'.) 36. Diving bird. 37. Ocelot. 38. 26. 39. Off it! (No such chess-man.) 40. Clan (gens) name. 41. Yes. (Four or more times, during the 9th century.) 42. Plague, 1665: Fire, 1666. 43. Genesis. 44. More. (1844.) 45. Venice. 46. 'Castling' (involving king and one rook.) 47. Mushrooms. 48. Switch 'fair' and 'brave'. 49. Yes. (Through Khyber Pass.) 50. More. (2.2 lbs.)

QUIZ 29

1. Amsterdam. 2. St Stephen. 3. S. American 'cowboys'. 4. None. (Greek, 'empty tomb'.) 5. (First) violin. 6. Alexander Graham Bell: (first words spoken over a telephone.) 7. A buccaneer. 8. Journalist. 9. (Vicious) fish. 10. None. (Spores produced under the leaves.) 11. The old. 12. Composer. 13. Snails. 14. Person retarded (by glandular deficiencies.) 15. Canasta. 16. Lindbergh. 17. Evaporate from solid to gas (without first melting.) 18. Serpent. (Serpere.) 19. Treatment of others. 20. Organized massacre. (Russia: usually directed against Jews.) 21. No. 22. Deliver, reviled. 23. 'Beaver!' 24. Jim (Hawkins.) 25. Musical. (Has 'bells'.) 26. Coal. 27. Starboard. 28. Ballet. 29. Cyprus. 30. (Latin, 'novem'.) 'Ninth hour' from sunrise! 31. Nova. 32. Salt paid to Roman soldiers. 33. The busy bee. 34. 'Ink' secreted by cuttlefish, etc. 35. Dance. (India.) 36. Quatre cinq, neuf. 37. Knick-knacks, artistic odds and ends. 38. Norway. 39. Epilogue. 40. God's. 41. Habeas corpus. 42. Charles II. 43. Burgomaster. 44. Nehru. 45. Discordant sound. 46. (One of the world's richest) art collections. 47. (Site owners) Knights Templars. 48. Kelvin. 49. No. (Record is 3 or 4 degrees below that.) 50. Shape. (Long, thinner.)

QUIZ 30

1. (Probably nothing, but) imagines himself ailing. 2. Irving. 3. Mount Elbruz. (Elbrus; 18,510 ft.) 4. (a) 4, (b) 6. 5. Transmutation. 6. Hoffman. 7. Galvanism. 8. Holman Hunt. 9. Acting. 10. Monaco. 11. (The god) Mercury. 12. Any bovine animal. 13. The Archer. 14. 'Benevolences'. 15. (a) Hanoi, (b) Saigon. 16. Fainting. 17. Ur. 18. Ignis fatuus, or will o' the wisps. 19. Scallop. 20. (Giuseppe) Verdi. 21. Bicycles have two: this has one. 22. The Goat. 23. Uranus. 24. Clown, fool. 25. Minim. 26. Urn. 27. New Zealand. (Clue, NZ.) 28. By air. 29. Arctic. 30. Glass. 31. Its front, or frontal aspect. 32. Being (or appearing to be) everywhere. 33. Reservoirs. 34. Nazarene. 35. Conductor. 36. They're pliant. 37. Charles Laughton. 38. Turner. 39. Bear, Slave. 40. Watches, clocks, measurement of time. 41. Italian cheeses. 42. Lawn tennis. 43. South Australia. 44. The gauntlet. 45. Seaweed. 46. Infra-red. 47. Guadeloupe. 48. Howitzer. 49. Yes. (In France.) 50. Cary Grant.

QUIZ 31

1. Mum. 2. Vasectomy. 3. Burdens; bundles to be carried. 4. Relapses into crime. 5. Banter. 6. Tetragon. (4-sided.) 7. East. 8. Oriental. 9. Terminus. 10. Sermon; discourse. 11. Cylinders. 12. Holland. 13. Convent (of Westminster.) 14. Brasil. 15. Poison gas. (World War I.) 16. Austin (friars.) 17. LL.D. 18. Maharajah, for one. 19. No. 20. Seven. 21. Cheese. (Swiss.) 22. Table Mountain. 23. Small. 24. 'Baked'. (Italian.) 25. Slight penetration, and then reflection, of light. 26. Song. 27. The Normandie. 28. Cross in corner: rest stripes: all in blue and white. 29. On top. 30. -itis. 31. Her right. 32. 'Iron bars a cage'. 33. Axis. 34. None. (Reflected sunlight.) 35. Mexico. 36. Felicitations. 37. Albert Finney. 38. 'If'. 39. Zinc. 40. Labels. 41. Beatitudes. 42. Papaya. 43. 'Potknocker's jellies are enjoyed by more people than any other brand'. (The jellies don't do the enjoying!) 44. Dickens' 'Tale of Two Cities'. 45. Helium. ('Helios'.) 46. St Paul's Cathedral. ('Great Paul'. nearly 17 tons.) 47. Aestivation. (Estivation.) 48. Poliomyelitis immunisation. 49. Injury, wound. 50. Helsingfors.

QUIZ 32

1. Gary Cooper. 2. 100. 3. Lethe: (lethal.) 4. The Scarlet Pimpernel. 5. Predicate. 6. Adam Smith. 7. Consensus. 8. 'Richard I'. 9. Medicinal substances. 10. Detroit! 11. The

Ancient Mariner. **12.** Excellent. **13.** Illicit diamond buying. **14.** Church. **15.** Henry VII. **15.** Tiber. **17.** Cooking too long. (Far more healthful, mineral-rich, steamed and slightly underdone.) **18.** None. (Locks, named for inventor: University for benefactor, ex-governor of Madras.) **19.** Obituary. **20.** About (1656.) **21.** 14 years. (14.2.) **22.** Rabbit. **23.** IM-peeus. **24.** Carnation. **25.** All used only once by individual popes. **26.** Gethsemane. **27.** (State of) Ohio. **28.** Soft. **29.** G. **30.** Ricochet. **31.** Australia. (About 6 million more.) **32.** Welcome. **33.** Pakistan. (Urdu.) **34.** Pitchblende. (Uraninite.) **35.** Skin (or other) reactions, (often due to allergies.) **36.** Play tympani. (Kettledrums.) **37.** (Douglas) fir. **38.** (Venetian, gold) coins. **39.** Earth's on the Moon. (Lunar eclipse.) **40.** (Ernest) Hemingway: Spencer Tracy. **41.** Norway. **42.** (Around) waist. (Sash.) **43.** 'Mary Pickford'. **44.** Cockleshells. **45.** Roumania. **46.** Taj Mahal. **47.** Far more likely to be! **48.** Pomegranate. (Not after 'Granada'.) **49.** Bergman. **50.** Lourdes, France.

QUIZ 33

1. (Jean Baptiste) Bernadotte. **2.** (Lake) Erie. **3.** Green, yellow. **4.** Ku Klux Klan. **5.** 'Take' piece, or pieces, offered. **6.** Buttermilk, skim-milk, whey. **7.** More. (Although number reduced by 75 per cent at first.) **8.** Hollywood. (Los Angeles.) **9.** Vestment. (Over alb and stole.) **10.** Onus. **11.** Colorado. **12.** (Casual) shoes or slippers. **13.** Lamination. **14.** (South Australia. (Largest there.) **15.** North. **16.** Pasteurization. **17.** (Shades of) brown (or yellow.) **18.** Nooses, moose, geese. **19.** 'To darkness and to me'. **20.** Pepsin. **21.** (Etienne de) Silhouette. **22.** Sign them. (Again, too, when cashing them.) **23.** Appendix, coccyx, larynx, etc. **24.** 'Hey diddle-diddle . . .' **25.** Town (Edirne) in Turkey: Hadrian. **26.** Manhattan. **27.** Panning. **28.** Cross of Lorraine. **29.** Sugar. **30.** Salt Lake City, Utah. **31.** Just about everything. (All forms of calcium carbonate.) **32.** No. (Oxidizes rapidly.) **33.** German divebombers. **34.** 'The Third Man'. **35.** Mint. **36.** 'These data are' or 'this datum is'. **37.** Carpenter. **38.** (The) Great Australian Bight. **39.** I, Belgium. II, Poland. **40.** No. (E.g. copper.) **41.** Apartheid. **42.** Tomorrow. **43.** (Inhaled and exhaled) 'air'. **44.** Horse. **45.** Mae West. **46.** Gambit. **47.** 'No-one may leave his or her seat'! ('No-one' is singular.) **48.** Yuri Gagarin. **49.** Tar. (Not nicotine!) **50.** Bacillus. (Means 'little rod'.)

QUIZ 34

1. Menservants. 2. Throwing over left shoulder. 3. 'Demons'. (Milton.) 4. Afrikaans. 5. Food. (Seeds.) 6. Sweden and Finland. 7. Golf, cricket, tennis, fencing. 8. Cheese. 9. Spectroscope. 10. Bone. 11. They're 'bent'. (E.g. appearance of stick partly immersed in water.) 12. Forearmed. 13. Marble. 14. Murmansk. 15. Times Square. 16. Maggot. 17. It isn't. ('Formed' from uranium.) 18. Ambidextrous. 19. Removal by cutting. (E.g. tonsillectomy.) 20. Lamas are monks. 21. Conspicuous, noticeable, etc. 32. Pancreas. 23. Mars. 24. Lash. 25. To 'fortune'. (If 'taken at the flood'.) 26. Mae West. 27. Temple, church, or weathercock. 28. Sherry. 29. Sea-shell; mollusc. (Conus gloriamaris; about 150 known.) 30. Tomorrow. 31. Eat that flaky roll or cake! 32. Affidavit. 33. Cape Cod. 34. Red, Black, Yellow, White. 35. Deciduous. (Sheds its needles.) 36. Capitulate. 37. Surface (mail, post.) 38. Hotels. Hilton. 39. Nickel. 40. Five farthings. 41. South American tea-like beverage; meat, or liver, paste. 42. St Luke. 43. Ash, beech, fir. 44. Richard Burton. 45. Nothing. 46. Helium. 47. (Including the Irtysh, one of world's longest) rivers. (Siberia.) 48. Left. 49. Their great height. 50. The Allies'.

QUIZ 35

1. Merry Christmas. 2. F. (32 degrees *below* freezing.) 3. Jupiter. 4. The bends. 5. Maxwelton. ('Annie Laurie'.) 6. Kaleidoscope. 7. Crème de Cacao. 8. Ottawa. 9. 'Heart'. 10. Lettuce. (Others Brassicaceae.) 11. Little Boy Blue. 12. New York. 13. Yalta. 14. Rio de Janeiro. 15. Axes. 16. Caduceus. 17. Samovars. 18. Research on fingerprints. 19. (a) Ferdinand, (b) Henry VII. 20. Caracas, Canberra, Cairo, Colombo, Copenhagen, Conakry. 21. 'Discs' (flexible cartilaginous sacs.) 22. A bar over it. (E.g. $\overline{XIV}$, 14,000.) 23. (Georgi) Malenkov. 24. Very definitely! 25. Chemically inactive. 26. (Union of) South Africa. 27. Convolvulus. 28. (Province of) New Brunswick. 29. O G K I C A Q. 30. Girls' names. 31. Washed hands. 32. Yes. (Called 'spat'.) 33. Quince. 34. Oranges. 35. 'HAY-nuss'. 36. Easy divorce. (When it was difficult elsewhere.) 37. Indian. 38. Virginia, and West Virginia. 39. Tony Curtis. 40. Sulphur. 41. Randolph. 42. New Orleans. (French background not as dominant as Montréal's.) 43. Gin rummy. 44. Regina. (Queen.) 45. Charles Darwin. 46. Pink. 47. Unnamed. 48. 'To enjoy soccer completely, etc.' 49. Shetland Is. 50. Banana.

QUIZ 36

1. The Jackdaw (of Rheims.) 2. Gases. (Minutely present in atmosphere.) 3. Its 'eye'. 4. Potsdam. 5. Bevel (led.) 6. To give a false alarm. 7. Sir Alexander Fleming. 8. Sherbert. ('Ice cream', made with fruit juice or flavouring, instead of cream.) 9. Lullaby, cradle-song. 10. Fiesta, siesta. 11. Argument, squabble. 12. Gunwhale. (Pronounced 'gunnel'.) 13. Electric light-bulb. 14. Kind of fruit. (Edible when a bit 'gone'.) 15. Lariat (or riata.) 16. 1917, 1941. 17. A, E, H, I, K, L, M, N, O, P, U, W. 18. Soya (soy) bean. 19. Lord Beaverbrook. 20. Columbus. 21. Lady Elizabeth Bowes-Lyon. 22. Siberia. (More than 90 degrees F. below zero.) 23. Cribbage. 24. Empire State Building. 25. Me. ('Object' of preposition.) 26. Pelican. 27. The White House. 28. Isle of Wight. 29. Peter. (Means 'rock'.) 30. New South Wales. 31. General Eisenhower and Sir Winston Churchill. 32. Tomato juice. 33. Moby Dick. (The white whale.) 34. P. G. Wodehouse. 35. Emulsion. 36. A moment. 37. Mexico. 38. Bits of gummed paper for mounting collected stamps. 39. Butcher, baker, and candlestick maker. 40. Badminton. 41. Mitre. 42. Ghana. 43. Swallow. (Nor a meal!) 44. Donkeys, horses, hyaenas, cattle. 45. Gazetteer. (Originally reference work for use by newsmen.) 46. (Large, globular, often wicker-covered) bottle. 47. Isolde. 48. Mustard. 49. May. 50. Hanged.

QUIZ 37

1. Mass parachute drop. 2. Wednesday. (Odin, Wodan.) 3. Moot. (As with a 'question', or 'point'.) 4. A pot of gold. 5. Brigadier-generals. 6. The law, crime. 7. Black Sea. 8. Easily crumbled. 9. Grow miniature, picturesquely stunted, trees. Japan. 10. 'Wossel'. 11. Single-celled animals. 12. Greece. 13. The scriptures. 14. Nitrogen. 15. Wales. 16. Joyful, joyous, jovial, jolly, jubilant. 17. Earthquakes. (Better name: tsunamis.) 18. Twice. (Six o'clock.) 19. First, opinion as to what's wrong. Second, opinion as to how it will all 'work out'. 20. Igneous. 21. 'Carbolic acid'. 22. Drink. 23. Belgium. 24. Ganges. 25. 'Charlie Chan'. 26. Isinglass. 27. Wane. 28. Florida. ('Indians'.) 29. Between 'toe and heel' of Italy. 30. Capacity, liquids. (Quarter of 'a barrel'.) 31. Passion play. 32. Orkneys. 33. Joshua. 34. Corona. 35. Iturbi. 36. Tobacco. 37. Fresco. 38. 12. 39. Fasces. (Origin of 'fascism'.) 40. Upright, ancient, monumental stone. 41. Kyoto. 42. Imperforate. 43. Vain whim, weak point in character. 44. Spermatozoa. 45. Flax. 46. Charles II. 47.

Eddie. (Elizabeth; Debbie.) 48. Sea. (Minerals heavier than water.) 49. 'Bing' Crosby. 50. Iberian.

QUIZ 38

1. (A different) fruit. 2. Manitoba. 3. Irrigation. 4. Deutschland. 5. (Either of a pair of shoulder) muscles. 6. Swinging like a pendulum.) 7. Same order as listed. 8. Former. 9. 1,024. 10. Inquest. 11. Yes. (Squint.) 12. Jelly-fish. (Hydrozoan coelenterate.) 13. Ida. 14. The Bank of England. 15. Yes. 16. Benjamin. 17. Hercule Poirot. 18. Amalgam. 19. Ducks. 20. Dog, (Russian wolf-hound.) 21. Death Valley, Cal. (Far below sea level.) 22. Alcohol. (Occasionally with ether.) 23. Ovine. 24. (The Three) Fates. 25. Hydrochloric. 26. Reynard. 27. 'San Fairey Ann' and 'Napoo'. 28. Wealth. 29. German armed forces. 30. Aster. (Gk. 'star'.) 31. (Lowly type of) plant. 32. Dopey. 33. 70. 34. Boasted; (about.) 35. Unicameral. (One-chambered.) 36. (Island group in) Indian. 37. Iambus, iambic. 38. Seven. 39. Mineral. (Hydrated magnesium silicate.) 'Sea-foam'. 40. Exaggeration. ('Got any beer?' 'Oceans of it!') 41. Durby. 42. Addis Ababa. (Ethiopia.) 43. Negates, contradicts, meaning. (E.g. 'septic', 'aseptic'.) 44. Five. 45. Envy-provoking, unjust. 46. Helicopter. 47. Unfading. (Or purple.) Either OK. 48. French Riviera (near Cannes.) 49. (Variously-sized) large wine bottles. 50. Nemesis.

QUIZ 39

1. All three. (Edward VI, Mary I, and Elizabeth I.) 2. Parachute. 3. Flanges. 4. Violins. 5. Aurelius. 6. Roumania. 7. Bar, to his Victoria Cross. 8. Denmark. (Greenland.) 9. Sri Lanka. 10. A word to the wise is sufficient. 11. Javelin. 12. Pinero. 13. The cat. 14. Norge. 15. Mauretania. 16. Geological periods. 17. Malmsey wine. 18. Bathos. 19. Nepal. 20. None. (Illusory, as in 'Arabian Nights' story.) 21. Zebra. 22. After a death, or at a funeral. 23. Margaret. (Also Marguerite.) 24. Members of various businessmen's service clubs. 25. Timur 'the Lame'. (Tamerlane.) 26. R. (Rho.) 27. Oswald. 28. Taking offence: feeling slighted. 29. Sauce-thickener of flour and fat. 30. (Smokeless) explosive (shaped like strings.) 31. Low-value coin. 32. Frog. 33. The aftermost one. 34. Weapons. (Curved Islamic sword.) 35. Invertebrates with many jointed legs. (E.g., insects, crustaceans.) 36. Dowels. 37. Lord Lister. (Aseptic, actually.) 38. Primogeniture. 39. Sarah Siddons. 40. (On a tenter, machine for)

stretching cloth. **41.** Dried. **42.** Oriental method of dyeing designs onto fabrics. **43.** (Marlowe's) 'Passionate Shepherd'. **44.** No. (N.Z. only.) **45.** Scylla. (Originally sea-monster.) **46.** Sons of Alphaeus and Zebedee, respectively. **47.** Tramp. **48.** Mucous membrane. **49.** Thoroughly. (Distilled from palm toddy, etc.) **50.** Oliver.

QUIZ 40
1. Once believed caused by 'bad air'. **2.** Safari. **3.** Phoenix. **4.** Hannibal. **5.** The escapement. **6.** Aztecs. **7.** Purdah. **8.** Colosseum at Rome. **9.** Demisemiquaver. **10.** Keats'. **11.** Censer. **12.** Afghanistan. **13.** Protective garments, for legs, worn by 'cowboys'. (Chaparejos.) **14.** Phrenologists. **15.** Thesaurus. **16.** Scion. **17.** Unfinished. **18.** One day. **19.** Shapeless (in any event!) **20.** A line drawn from any point to its centre. **21.** Parma. **22.** Fire. **23.** Scalp. **24.** Styles of printing type. **25.** Tendrils. **26.** Tumbrils. (Dung carts.) **27.** Peregrine. **28.** Mauritius. (1847); (UK 1840.) **29.** On soft palate (over back of tongue.) **30.** Epstein. **31.** Egg-plant. **32.** Nigeria. **33.** Nitre. **34.** Solstice. (In June, and December.) **35.** Calabash. **36.** Protoplasm. **37.** Skye. **38.** Aloes. **39.** Marmalade. ('Marmelo'.) **40.** Wilderness. **41.** Saladin. **42.** Celluloid. **43.** Sweden. **44.** Velasquez. **45.** Baku. **46.** St John. **47.** Armpit. **48.** Sir Harry Lauder. **49.** 'Limbo'. **50.** Vineyard.